First World War
and Army of Occupation
War Diary
France, Belgium and Germany

29 DIVISION
Divisional Troops
147 Brigade Royal Field Artillery
1 March 1916 - 31 December 1916

WO95/2292/2

The Naval & Military Press Ltd
www.nmarchive.com
Published in association with The National Archives

Published by

The Naval & Military Press Ltd

Unit 10 Ridgewood Industrial Park,

Uckfield, East Sussex,

TN22 5QE England

Tel: +44 (0) 1825 749494

www.naval-military-press.com

www.nmarchive.com

This diary has been reprinted in facsimile from the original. Any imperfections are inevitably reproduced and the quality may fall short of modern type and cartographic standards.

© **Crown Copyright**
Images reproduced by permission of The National Archives, London, England, 2015.

Contents

Document type	Place/Title	Date From	Date To
Heading	WO95/2292/2 147 Brigade Royal Field Artillery		
Heading	29th Division Troops Divl Artillery 147th Brigade R.F.A. Mar 1916-Dec 1916 Became Afa Rt Bde Jan 1917 To 1. Army		
Heading	??		
Heading	147 Bde R F A Vol I B E F From M E F Fourth Army		
War Diary	Suez Camp	01/03/1916	09/03/1916
War Diary	Alexandria	11/03/1916	11/03/1916
War Diary	At Sea	12/03/1916	17/03/1916
War Diary	Marseilles	18/03/1916	18/03/1916
War Diary	Entrained	19/03/1916	21/03/1916
War Diary	Villers Sous Ailly	22/03/1916	31/03/1916
Miscellaneous	The Officer i/c Adjustant General Office Base B.E.F.		
Heading	29th Division 147th Brigade R.F.A. April 1916		
Heading	147 Bde R F A Vol II		
War Diary	Domart	01/04/1916	03/04/1916
Miscellaneous	Sutdy the Last-mentioned Battery in 17/5 Brigade RFA Is 92nd Not 97th		
Miscellaneous	Ordered by Br. General Jackson at 11.10 a.m. to reinforce and prolong the line to the		
War Diary	Domart	04/04/1916	09/04/1916
War Diary	Amplier	09/04/1916	16/04/1916
War Diary	Englebelmer	16/04/1916	26/04/1916
War Diary	Mailly Mallet	27/04/1916	30/04/1916
Miscellaneous	From Lieut-General Sir Aylmer Hunter Weston K.C.B. D.S.O.	25/04/1916	25/04/1916
Heading	29th Division 147th Brigade R.F.A. May 1916		
Miscellaneous	To D.A.G. 3rd Echelon	11/06/1916	11/06/1916
War Diary	Mailly-Maillet	01/05/1916	31/05/1916
Heading	29th Division 147th Brigade R.F.A. June 1916		
Heading	War Diary of 147th Brigade R F A From June 1st 1916 To June 30th 1916 (Volume 10)		
War Diary		01/06/1916	30/06/1916
War Diary	U Day	24/06/1916	24/06/1916
War Diary	V Day	25/06/1916	25/06/1916
War Diary	W Day	26/06/1916	26/06/1916
War Diary	X Day	27/06/1916	27/06/1916
War Diary	'Y' Day	28/06/1916	30/06/1916
Heading	29th Division 147th Brigade R.F.A. July 1916		
War Diary	In The Field	01/07/1916	31/07/1916
Heading	29th Division 147th Brigade R.F.A. August 1916		
War Diary		01/08/1916	31/08/1916
Heading	29th Division. 147th Brigade R.F.A. September 1916		
Heading	War Diary of 147th Brigade RFA From 1/9/16 To 30/9/16 (Volume 12)		
War Diary	France	01/09/1916	03/09/1916
Miscellaneous			
War Diary		03/09/1916	03/09/1916
War Diary	France	03/09/1916	15/09/1916
War Diary	Belgium	15/09/1916	30/09/1916

Heading	29th Division. 147th Brigade R.F.A. October 1916		
Heading	War Diary 147th Brigade R F A From Oct 1st 1916 To Oct 31st 1916 (Volume 14)		
War Diary	Ypres	01/10/1916	09/10/1916
War Diary	March To The Somme District	10/10/1916	13/10/1916
War Diary	Somme Front	13/10/1916	31/10/1916
Heading	29th Division 147th Brigade R.F.A. November 1916		
Heading	War Diary 147th Brigade RFA From Nov 1st To Nov 30th (Volume)		
War Diary	Vicinity of Longueval	01/11/1916	24/11/1916
War Diary	Locality of Longueval	25/11/1916	25/11/1916
War Diary	E 28 Near Meaultel	26/11/1916	28/11/1916
War Diary	A.I.D.	29/11/1916	30/11/1916
Heading	29th Division. 147th Brigade R.F.A. December 1916		
Heading	War Diary 147th Brigade RFA Dec 1st To Dec 31st (Vol 10)		
War Diary	A.I.D In Vicinity Of Montauban	01/12/1916	05/12/1916
War Diary	Map France 57c S.W. H.Q. At T 20 D 4.0 Battery In Vicinity Of T. 16	06/12/1916	17/12/1916
War Diary	Map France 57.c S.W. H.Q. T.20 d.40 Battery Position In Vicinity Of T.16	18/12/1916	23/12/1916
War Diary	Map France 57c S.W. H.Q. T20 d.40 Battery in Vicinity Of T.16	24/12/1916	26/12/1916
War Diary	Map France 57.c S.W. H.Q. T.20 d.40 Battery Position In Vicinity Of T.16	27/12/1916	31/12/1916

WO95/2292/2

B 147 Brigade Royal Field Artillery

29TH DIVISION TROOPS
DIV: ARTILLERY

147TH BRIGADE R.F.A.

MAR 1916-DEC 1916

Became A F Art Bde
JAN 1917 to I. ARMY

29

14 y Bde R.F.A.

Vol I BEF
from MEF

Fourth Army

ORIGINAL
Army Form C. 2118.

107 Brigade

WAR DIARY
—or—
INTELLIGENCE SUMMARY.
(Erase heading not required.)

Place	Date	Hour	Summary of Events and Information	Remarks and references to Appendices
Lucknow Camp			The day was bright and hot. Lieut Col. Drummond-Hay left for Port Said to embark on the "Llandovery Castle" for Marseilles.	
			The 15th Brigade RHA & 17th Brigade RFA witnessed their complement of wagons limbers & telephone wagons from our gun parks.	
			All units of this Brigade wanted painting the new guns uniform, which are not complete account & establishment.	
	2		Wind from South causing bad sand storm. General Smith came down from Ismailia & rode round the camps. Col. Hine-Haycock Remount Officer was expected but did not come down. The 460th How. Battery marched out entrained for Alexandria. We drew 2 horses and 35 mules from the 88th Infantry Brigade Transport & also 8 horses from the 460th How Battery which were posted as follows:—	
			10th Battery 6 horses 9 mules	
			97th " 10 "	
			368th " 4 10 "	
			A.C. 7 "	

WAR DIARY
or
INTELLIGENCE SUMMARY.
(Erase heading not required.)

Army Form C. 2118.

Place	Date	Hour	Summary of Events and Information	Remarks and references to Appendices
Suez Camp	Mar. 3		Work continues from SOUTH stand very bad.	
			Wt drew 3 horses 460 mules from the 88th Infantry Brigade Transport which were posted as follows:-	
			10th Battery — 18 mules	
			97th " — 18 "	
			368th " — 19 "	
			A.C. — 6 "	
			Also 28 mules complete with harness from the 29th Divisional Train A.S.C. of which 4 were posted to Head Quarters for the Telephone Wagon the remainder to 10th Battery.	
			Comdg IX Corps	
			The Corps Commander General Sir FRANCIS DANES, came round the Camps of the Division to say 'farewell'.	
		4	Hot wind continues blowing strongly from SOUTH stand still very bad.	
			Wt drew the following mules with harness from the 29th Divisional Train A.S.C. from the 86th Infantry Brigade Transport without harness.	
				14 mules from 86 Inf Bt T
			10th Battery — 3 mules from 29th Div T.	1 horse 12 " "
			97th " — 28 " " " "	14 " "
			368th " — 27 " " " "	
			A.C. — 2 " " " "	

Army Form C. 2118.

WAR DIARY
or
INTELLIGENCE SUMMARY.
(Erase heading not required.)

Place	Date	Hour	Summary of Events and Information	Remarks and references to Appendices
Camp	Feb. 4		up to date the mules drawn from the 29th Divisional Train are of a good stamp, fine things, in good condition, easily handled great well, but those from the Infantry transport are smaller & really too light for the work required rendered to give more transfer in handling we have on its take 4 50 000 rounds S.A.A. when we arrive at ALEXANDRIA to embark. Four D.A.C. Scouts which were sent to Ordnance at ISMAILIA for rifles. Major Stewart 48th Howr. Battery R.G.A. with two 9·2 guns marched on Captain K.M. BAIN O.C. 91 Battery, returned from leave to ENGLAND.	
	5		Day very hot & close — Church parade was held at 10 30 am for the Divisional Artillery. All units of the Brigade drew the following ammunition from Ordnance:—	

	Eng. Per	Shrapnel	H.E.
10th Battery	573	29	163
97th "	666		152
368th	564		140
Amm. Col.	634		228

Capt. HODGKINSON and Lieut. POWELL returned to proceed to ALEXANDRIA & report to D.A.G. 3rd Echelon they return (in the evening) will have more details off from

Army Form C. 2118.

WAR DIARY
or
INTELLIGENCE SUMMARY.
(Erase heading not required.)

Place	Date	Hour	Summary of Events and Information	Remarks and references to Appendices
Surg Camp Nov	5		The advanced party of 62 men marched out at 1 am this morning to entrain for ALEXANDRIA when they are to embark on the "MINNETOO" for MARSEILLES. Lieut. E.L. KIDD was ordered to stop behind, instructions would be sent to Lieut. DRUMMOND-HAY to take charge of the party at their destination. The day hot down but little dust, flies becoming very bad.	
	6		97th Battery exchanged 92 rounds Shrapnel for HE with 17th Brigade RFA. A draft of 47 men marched in at 21.30, composed of 30 Gunners & 17 Drivers. Day was hot and windy.	
	7		We sent 3 wagon loaders and 2 wagons with 162 rounds Shrapnel 85 fuze to EL KUBRI and exchanged with 42nd Lowland Division for 80 fuze. 2nd Lieut R.M. DALE was posted to this Brigade as supernumerary officer & attached to 97th Battery from the 15th Brigade RFA. The day was hot rainy sand bad.	
	8		The 15th Brigade RFA commenced to march out at about 5 pm to entrain for ALEXANDRIA and were followed by the 15th Brigade RFA.	
	9		Cool morning but changed to hot wind but cloudy. 90th Heavy Battery (160 plus), marched in.	

Army Form C. 2118.

WAR DIARY
or
INTELLIGENCE SUMMARY.
(Erase heading not required.)

Place	Date	Hour	Summary of Events and Information	Remarks and references to Appendices
Suez Camp.	Feb. 9.		All available officers of the Brigade rode out about five miles NW of SUEZ with General STOCKDALE to reconnoitre position for sham fight to take place the following day at which Sir ARCHIBALD MURRAY is to be present. On return found orders to entrain the next day for ALEXANDRIA. Night very much colder, day very hot.	
	10		14th Siege Battery marched in — Left. The 10th & 368th Batteries entrained for port train at 19.20 and 40 & 97th Ammunition Column & 1140 left on second train at 22.20 for ALEXANDRIA. Morning cold & very wet — Afternoon fine & rain normal. The 10 & 369th Batteries & HQ entrained on HT "EXCELLE" for Marseilles. The 91st Battery Ammunition Column went to GABBARI rest camps to await later conveyance. On the same transport 20th HQ of 132nd Howr. Brigade & Y battery (late 460th Howr Battery) embarked.	
Alexandria	11		The Brigade has 189 horses from remounts of which 19 were Belgian. Had great difficulty to complete establishment remounts arrived mostly in driblets. These included batches of officers chargers which were 550 dollars per animal. All horses, with 52 mules, were embarked on ship and well ventilated trough[?] or matting arrangement, but difficult to ensure	

WAR DIARY
or
INTELLIGENCE SUMMARY
(Erase heading not required.)

Army Form C. 2118.

Hour, Date, Place	Summary of Events and Information	Remarks and references to Appendices
May 11.	No parade except in charge of the central park. The following officers were embarked :- **1st Brigade RFA Headquarters** Lt. Col. D.E. FORMAN (O.C. Troops) Lieut. A.M. McCRACKEN (Ship's Adjutant) " C.R. ROCHÉ (Veterinary officer) 2nd Lieut. G.G. GRIFFITH-WILLIAMS O.R. 36. Horses 28. Mules 5. Vehicles 2. including 2 men and 2 mules with limber g.s. wagon belonging to DAMR. **10th Battery.** Capt. J. & H.C. BATTEN Lieut. A. BINNIE " K.R. PARK " W.J. NOWELL O.R. 114. Horses 73. Mules 57. Vehicles 12. **368th Battery.** Lieut. C.H. CALVERT " F.J.A. HART " A.F. LEIGHTON O.R. 129. Horses 63. Mules 68. Vehicles 12. **97th Battery.** O.R. 19.	

Army Form C. 2118.

WAR DIARY
or
INTELLIGENCE SUMMARY
(Erase heading not required.)

Instructions regarding War Diaries and Intelligence Summaries are contained in F. S. Regs., Part II. and the Staff Manual respectively. Title pages will be prepared in manuscript.

Hour, Date, Place	Summary of Events and Information	Remarks and references to Appendices
Mch. 11.	132nd How. Brigade RFA Headquarters. Lieut. Col. H.R.W. MARRIOTT SMITH Lieut. T.J. CURNISON Lieut. J.C. LISTER Capt. J.R. ALLEN R.A.M.C. O.R. 23 Horses 19 "C" Battery (late 460th How. Batty.) Major J.M. GIBBON Lieut. M. STAVELEY Lieut. G.P. DUFF. " J. STEWART. O.R. 132 Horses 125. Mules 105 Vehicles 12. Details A & B Batteries O.C. W. [?] Took three officers and schedule without remainder left 29 animals to allow spare stalls. Fine sunset. Getting cold but sea normal. Lunch off Malta about 02.30 Forward to proceed at [?] 07.00. All lits [?] fine sunset.	
At Sea Mch 14/14		
" 15		
" 16		

Army Form C. 2118.

WAR DIARY
or
INTELLIGENCE SUMMARY
(Erase heading not required.)

Instructions regarding War Diaries and Intelligence Summaries are contained in F.S. Regs., Part II. and the Staff Manual respectively. Title pages will be prepared in manuscript.

Hour, Date, Place	Summary of Events and Information	Remarks and references to Appendices
After Marseilles	Cool and fine weather. Several halts beginning to feel change of climate and want of exercise. Arrived off MARSEILLES at 21.00	
Marseilles – 18.	Dull but fine. Snow near during night. Orders to entrain for PONT REMY first train left at 19.30 with all the vehicles. 1 Officer left at 21.15 in an Infantry train with the animals. Other Brigade personnel. Officers' Mess left at 11.30 Bge is big unit experiencing difficulty.	
Entrained 19.	H.Q. and F.A. Brigade left three hours in hospital at MARSEILLES. Bright and fine. Dull with soft rain.	
21	Cold and wet. Arrived PONT REMY at 03.00 and detrained immediately. Was instructed to ABT when Bge Hd Qrs and 368th Battery are and III to billet at VILLERS 368 Bur and 11+ 363 Battery moved on to VAUCHELLES	Note:— VILLERS about 6 miles beyond from PONT REMY. VAUCHELLES about 2 mile further on beyond VILLERS.

2/Lt K.R. Pickette fell on him & was removed to Hospital
MAJOR H. DENISON afforded 368th Battery at MOUFFLERS vice CAPT _____
2/Lt BATE at MOUFFLERS

This was "A" Battery 188th Brigade and arrived in France from England on 13th March 1916. Its formation dates from Aug. 1915. This Battery possesses exceptionally fine stock of draught horses.

WAR DIARY or INTELLIGENCE SUMMARY

Army Form C. 2118.

Hour, Date, Place	Summary of Events and Information	Remarks and references to Appendices
VILLES-SOUS-AILLY March 22 1916	Wet and cold. Lieut. R.M. DALE attached to 10th Battery. The 9th Battery and Ammunition Column marched to hillabout VILLERS-SOUS-AILLY. Returned later g.o. wagon, 2 men and 2 mules to DAH QM. Took over 1st line transport from R.A. Section ASSEVILLE consisting of: 5 mm carts (one for each unit), 5 water ", 1 Mother " (Eng. HQ), 2 G.S. wagons (in A.C.), 8 G.S. wagons " ", limbered and 129 animals.	Billets - very bad; horse 3 miles from billets. Troop horses & mules picketted in open, only officers chargers under cover.
23	Cold and wet. Lieut. F.H. ORR posted to 10th Battery. 2/Lieut. R.M. DALE attached to QM. Two sections of R.A.M.C. arrived from first scheme. Brigadier General STOCKDALE, D.S.O. went home on leave with Lt. Col. M.P. MONKHOUSE, C.M.G., M.V.O. assume command of brigade artillery.	
24	Showery & mainly. Field Cashier came to Headquarters and paid.	

WAR DIARY
or
INTELLIGENCE SUMMARY

(Erase heading not required.)

Army Form C. 2118.

Hour, Date, Place	Summary of Events and Information	Remarks and references to Appendices
VILLERS-COTTAUX March 25.1916.	Snowed but cleared from later. A.C. returned 3 limbers & 5 wagons to R.A. Section at ROISEVILLE owing to modification in Establishment. A.T. drew 346,000 rounds S.A.A. from dump at PONT REMY Lieut R.R. PARK rejoined 10th Battery from hospital at Experimentary officers. Lieut MIERMEN & Lieut CALVERT repty of 8 men proceeded on ten days leave to England.	
" 26.	Fine & kindly. 80 animals sent to 15th Arm Brigade at PONT REMY ... Remnts for 80 good mules & A.C. Lieut WYLIE and party of 3 men proceeded home on leave Lt Col FORMAN empld to work malaria Hosp. 4 DIVISION assuming temporary command of the Brigade.	
" 27.	Passed all day. Lieut R.R. ROCHE AV.C. returned to Unit for duty. Lieut A.BOURNE party of 3 men proceeded home on leave A.T. drew 407 rounds Shrapnel from dump at PONT REMY to Brigade now being supplied in regular shipments + Sm each Brigade now being supplied in regular shipments + 607 rounds shell of H.E. & wheat ammo at dump.	

WAR DIARY
or
INTELLIGENCE SUMMARY

(Erase heading not required.)

Army Form C. 2118.

Hour, Date, Place	Summary of Events and Information	Remarks and references to Appendices
VILLERS sous AILLY Mch 27	The Brigade sent in 20 sick, wounded & wasted to Hospital at Pont Remy and 56 spare mounts to Remounts at ABBEVILLE.	
28	Army ordinary. Lieut. CLAYTON-BARKER party of 3 proceeded to England on leave. Lt-Col. FORMAN admitted to No 3 Casualty Clearing Station. Lt or OWEN with Malaria. A.C. Ford motor cycle from Remt failure. German Raiding party left St GERMAINCOURT when Kent NoWELL admitted Bulleting in the morning. Snowed during the afternoon advised that Lord KITCHENER would be in this area today. Popped Scott mounted on mule marching parties to LONG and back via BOUCHON animals went very well. 9 Y.H. Battery and one horse to Hospital.	
29	Army in field. 9 Y.H. Battery sent him horses to Hospital. Received orders to move to district of devonain day.	

WAR DIARY
or
INTELLIGENCE SUMMARY
(Erase heading not required.)

Army Form C. 2118.

Hour, Date, Place	Summary of Events and Information	Remarks and references to Appendices
VILLERS sous AILLY March 31st 1918.	Day was bright and warm. Brigade HQrs, 91st & 368th Batteries and Ammunition Column marched out at 09.30 with instructions to the C in C roads under L of LA FOLIE AUBERGE (AMIENS 12. J 50 cm) at 10.30 and to put in behind the 15th R.H.A. Brigade on CO LETOILE/DOMART and the 10th and 371st Batteries under the remainder of the brigade at the East Road from FAUCHELLE and MOUFLERS respectively. So 15th Brigade himself up there the whole Division Artillery was placed in DOMART EN PONTHIEU & 132 this Brigade having arrived the day before from PONT REMY. The 91st Battery left the Rhine Bomber in case of the range at VILLERS in charge and instructions from the Veterinary officer. Billets at DOMART a great improvement on those just evacuated; whole Brigade all together. Unfortunately Troop horse facilities for watering bad, as usually Troop horse fronts picketted in the open officers accommodation not in fort.	D Somm... Lt Col BuRFA Com 147 Bde RFA

Confidential

The Officer.
i/c Adjutant General's Office
Base. B.E.F.

29th Division.

147th BRIGADE

R. F. A.

APRIL 1 9 1 6

29

147 Bde R.F.A.
―――――――
Vol II

Original

Army Form C. 2118.

Sheet I

WAR DIARY
or
INTELLIGENCE SUMMARY
(Erase heading not required.)

Instructions regarding War Diaries and Intelligence Summaries are contained in F. S. Regs., Part II. and the Staff Manual respectively. Title pages will be prepared in manuscript.

Hour, Date, Place	Summary of Events and Information	Remarks and references to Appendices

Domart - April 1.

1. The day was fine and mild. The gun teams were parked alongside helps now in field. The horses were on the open and picketed in farm close in the neighbourhood. On the whole rather better than at VILLERS-SOUS-AILLY. The billets for officers were scanty due to the whole Divisional Artillery being in the one village what rather attained its reserves. The 93rd Infantry Brigade marched through their way to FIENVILLERS.

2. The weather continued fine warm. Rations to-day drawn from the ASC dump at BERNEUIL. A supply of stores arrived & were packed as follows:—

    10th Battery   6.
    91   "   6.
    368   "   6.
    A.C. -   5
                   ——
                   23.

3. Fine warm. Colonel FORMAN returned from hospital and assumed command of the troops in DOMART as Divisional Artillery Headquarters less the Staff Captain, moved on to ACHEUX. An advance party of the 15th Brigade RFA, 147th and 132nd Brigades R.F.A. also proceeded to ACHEUX, the H.Q. of the 29th Division

Surely the last-mentioned Battery in 17th Brigade RFA is 92nd NOT 97th? JBS

companies in reserve behind it had been

ordered by Br.-General Jackson at 11.10 a.m.

to reinforce and prolong the line to the

Original

Instructions regarding War Diaries and Intelligence Summaries are contained in F.S. Regs., Part II. and the Staff Manual respectively. Title pages will be prepared in manuscript.

Army Form C. 2118.

Sheet II

WAR DIARY
or
INTELLIGENCE SUMMARY
(Erase heading not required.)

Hour, Date, Place	Summary of Events and Information	Remarks and references to Appendices
DOMART April 4th	The day was cold and overcast.	
" 5th	The weather continued cold and dull. The following Batteries marched out to take up their new MAILLY MAILLET and ENGLEBELMER:—	
	15th Brigade RFA. 14th Brigade RFA. 132nd Brigade RFA. (How.)	
	One section "B" Battery. 13th Battery. A/132 Battery (late 460th)	
	— Y — 26 "	
		97 "
" 6th	Continued cold and dull. 149th Brigade Headquarters moved into the Chateau at DOMART. Lieuts. A.M. McCRACKEN and CALVERT and 7 men returned from leave in ENGLAND. Ordered to send an officer and interpreter to FRESCHVILLERS and VAMPLIER to arrange billets for the remainder of the artillery still in DOMART consisting of :—	
	147th Brigade RFA complete.	
	15th " RHA. One section "B" Battery, 369th Battery and Am. Col.	
	14th " RFA. 370th " " " "	
	132nd " RFA. 13/132 and 9/132 Batteries " " "	
" 7th	Weather continued cold and rainy. Lieut. J.B.B. MARTIN from Ammunition Column sent to hospital - pile.	

Original

Army Form C. 2118.

Sheet 3

WAR DIARY
or
INTELLIGENCE SUMMARY

(Erase heading not required.)

Instructions regarding War Diaries and Intelligence Summaries are contained in F. S. Regs., Part II. and the Staff Manual respectively. Title pages will be prepared in manuscript.

Hour, Date, Place	Summary of Events and Information	Remarks and references to Appendices
DOMART April 7th Cont.	received a party of 4 officers and 34 other ranks to VALHEUREUX for a course of instruction with Trench Mortars;

10th Battery   2nd Lieut. K.R. PARK   and   10 O.R. — Indians }
97 "   "   H.M. MEREWETHER   10 "   2 officers}
368 "   Lieut. F.J.A. HART   10 "   8 "   Servants
371 "   Lieut. H.M. HEATH   8 "

On the return of the horses of the 371st Battery fell dead. | Approved march |
| 8th | The day was bright but still cold. Ordered to send a billeting party to AMPLIER which proceeded under 2nd Lieut. NOWELL, and the remainder of the Artillery left at DOMART to march tomorrow. | |
| 9th | Weather was fine & bright. During the stay at DOMART efforts were made to complete the needs of the Brigade for material, clothing etc., from Ordnance, who had moved from LONG to CANDAS and later to ACHEUX, but with very little success, and not the least serious. The lack of shoes for both mules & horses. At 0900 the Brigade marched out from DOMART for AMPLIER leaving four horses behind too lame to march. | |

Original

Army Form C. 2118.
Sheet 4

WAR DIARY
or
INTELLIGENCE SUMMARY
(Erase heading not required.)

Instructions regarding War Diaries and Intelligence Summaries are contained in F.S. Regs., Part II. and the Staff Manual respectively. Title pages will be prepared in manuscript.

Hour, Date, Place	Summary of Events and Information	Remarks and references to Appendices
AMPLIER, April 9th cont.	The route chosen was via BERNEUIL, MONTRELET and BEAUVAL a distance of about 15 miles and round CANDAS.	
	On arrival, the congested roads round CANDAS. The guns wagons were parked in the open by Three Hills being distributed as few as possible with Kineties. The lines were picketed to the open & the men put into shells built of a light framework about 15 by 10 covered with canvas in a light framework. Only a few officers were billeted in the village, The remainder in some sort of sheds against the main road.	
	VIIIth Corps passed through in the afternoon but did not inspect the Brigade owing to Gen Hunter-Weston KCB DSO commanding. The only men marched in the valley afforded foulities for watering horses & mules were sent down by the A.T.C.	
	Weather continues fine.	
10th	2/Lieut A.L. WYLIE 975 Battery returned from leave in ENGLAND	
	The Brigade was ordered to send a digging party to report to D.A.H.Q. at ACHEUX which marched out under Captain HETHERINGTON and was composed of the following: —	
	10th Battery Lieut GRAY and 2/Lieut NOWELL + 49 O.R.	
	97 " " COSTELLO " + 46 O.R.	
	368 " " CALVERT " LEIGHTON + 40 O.R.	
	371 " " BEECHER & 40 O.R.	
	A.C. Lieut PIERSON " DALE " 21 O.R.	

Original

Army Form C. 2118.

Sheet V

WAR DIARY
or
INTELLIGENCE SUMMARY
(Erase heading not required.)

Instructions regarding War Diaries and Intelligence Summaries are contained in F.S. Regs, Part II. and the Staff Manual respectively. Title pages will be prepared in manuscript.

Hour, Date, Place	Summary of Events and Information	Remarks and references to Appendices
AMPLIER April 11th	Weather became very wet and cold. Lieut. CLAYTON BARKER returned from leave. Captain HETHERINGTON reports front very quiet and digging party divided to that the parties from 371st Battery and A.C. are working on positions of 15th Bryade R.H.A. ~~~~~~~ near MAILLY MALLET and remainder on our own positions near ENGLEBELMER.	
" 12th	Continued cold and very wet. Lt. Col. FORMAN went home on leave, Major DENISON, 368th Battery assumed command. Sent waggons from Head-Quarters to digging party. Baggage slightly beyond returned to H.Q. Divisional Train. Cold and wet. Lieut. L.E. PAINTER posted on 10th instant attached R 10th A.C. " 9th " - . " W.C. ROBINSON " " " " " " -	
" 13th	Weather continues wet year.	
" 14th	Lieuts. MEREWETHER and PARK returned from course of instruction in Trench Mortars at PALHEUREUX. Lieut HART and 2Lieut HEATH were sent forward to the trenches together with Y Battery medium Trench Mortars the first named being in command; the 34 O.R.s were divided up amongst the various Trench Mortar Batteries. 2Lieut PAINTER proceeded to HAVERNAS for course of gunnery.	

Original

WAR DIARY
or
INTELLIGENCE SUMMARY
(Erase heading not required.)

Army Form C. 2118.

Sheet 6

Instructions regarding War Diaries and Intelligence Summaries are contained in F. S. Regs., Part II. and the Staff Manual respectively. Title pages will be prepared in manuscript.

Hour, Date, Place	Summary of Events and Information	Remarks and references to Appendices
AMPLIER. April 15th	The day was wet and cold.	
16th	The horses of the Brigade were taken for shelter. Head Quarters moved to move tomorrow to ENGLEBELMER. The weather improved & the day was bright & fine. Lieut. J.G.B. MARTIN returned from hospital. Head Quarters moved to ENGLEBELMER, about 13 miles.	
ENGLEBELMER.	The village was overcrowded and billets were poor and hard to arrange. Spare horses from Brigade at Bolle Eglise of which 3 were parked with the 371st Battery and one to each of the remaining units of the Brigade.	BELLE EGLISE
17th	Turned wet again.	
18th	Wet and cold. Colonel FORMAN returned from leave owing to all officers being recalled. Lieut. L.H. Calvert 368th Battery appointed Staff Captain to Trench Mortar Group, 29th Division.	
19th	Wet and cold.	
20th	Showery. 10th Battery B.C. Staff arrived from AMPLIER.	

Original

Army Form C. 2118.

Sheet 7

WAR DIARY
or
INTELLIGENCE SUMMARY
(Erase heading not required.)

Hour, Date, Place	Summary of Events and Information	Remarks and references to Appendices
ENGLEBELMER April 21.19.16.	Morning was fine but wet again in the afternoon. A draft of 23 men from the D.A.C. arrived and were posted to 10th Battery " " " 8 " " " " 36th " " " " 4 " " " " 97th " Orders were received to send the 37th Battery into action near SAILLY AU BOIS and report to Colonel GOSSETT, R.F.A., Commdg S. MIDLAND Brigade R.F.A., 48th Division. Every available man was put onto hauling the 10th Battery's position at X1; material for overhead cover was drawn from Zt. 17th Brigade Park from two disused gun pits about Q.16a, 2030 (map BEAUMONT 57dSW). Position also ACHEUX and from R.E. dump at COURCELLES.	
22.	The day was wet and cold. Brigadier General R.A. 29th Division, General STEENDALE D.S.O. was relieved by General Malcolm PEAKE, C.M.G.	
23.	Showery but weather improving 10th Battery marched in from AMPLIER and put three guns in position during the night of the 23/24th.	
24.	The day was fine. 2nd Lt. ROBINSON and four men detailed to a course at BERTRANCOURT for distinguishing aeroplanes. 10th Battery wagon lines at ENGLEBELMER in an orchard.	

Original

Army Form C. 2118.

Sheet 1

WAR DIARY
or
INTELLIGENCE SUMMARY
(Erase heading not required.)

Instructions regarding War Diaries and Intelligence Summaries are contained in F. S. Regs., Part II. and the Staff Manual respectively. Title pages will be prepared in manuscript.

Hour, Date, Place	Summary of Events and Information	Remarks and references to Appendices

ENGLEBELMER April 24 Cont. The 371st Battery came into action (right section only) at K 20 d 20.00 (Map HEBUTERNE 1/10,000) at 21.55.

25 The day was spent.

Announcing of the landing in Gallipoli and received congratulatory messages from Lieut. Gen. Sir AYLMER HUNTER-WESTON K.C.B., D.S.O. (attached).

Colonel FORMAN to command LEFT Group Divisional Artillery and Colonel MONKHOUSE RIGHT GROUP.

Left Group consists of "B", "L", & "Y" Batteries R.H.A. 369th Battery R.F.A comprising 1.5 Brigade R.H.A, "B" & "C" Batteries 132nd Hvy Bugade R.F.A, 97th + 368th " 147th Bugade R.F.A
The 10th + 371st Batteries will be under Colonel MONKHOUSE for tactical purposes.

Lieuts. A.L. WYLIE and J.B.B. MARTIN ordered to Trench Mortar School at VALHEUREUX for a course of instruction with a view to relieve Lieut. HART and HEATH.

10th Battery fired 120 rounds Shrapnel in registering a piece of wire at PHANTHORN REDOUBT.

371st Battery fired 15 rounds Shrapnel to register K 12 a 00 80
 "   8 "   "   "   "   "   "   "   "   "   "
 "   10 "   "   "   "   "   "   "   " K 11 c 65 80

1247 W 3299 200,000 (E) 8/14 J.B.C. &A. Forms/C. 2118/11.

Army Form C. 2118.

Sheet 9

WAR DIARY
or
INTELLIGENCE SUMMARY
(Erase heading not required.)

Hour, Date, Place	Summary of Events and Information	Remarks and references to Appendices
ENGLEBELMER April 26	Day very fine and warm. Head quarters of the Brigade moved to MAILLY MAILLET a more convenient and central place for left group. 371st Battery fired 24 rounds Shrapnel to register K12a00.30	
MAILLY MAILLET " 27	Bright and fine weather. 16th Battery fired 26 rounds Shrapnel to register a point on HAWTHORNE REDOUBT. 371st Battery did not fire.	
" 28	Day was fine and warm. 2/Lieut. M.O. HASKELL posted to the Brigade and attached to the 368th Battery. Grew more material for gun positions. 10th Battery still needing overhead cover and 368th and 97th Batteries very backward and 371st new position not started. All these Batteries are in the open on rolling ground to the EAST of ENGLEBELMER. 10th Battery fired 14 rounds Shrapnel to register on HAWTHORN REDOUBT. 371st " 19 " " " front Trench K11a80.60.	
" 29	Day was bright and fine. 2/Lieut. E.E. CATTELL posted to Brigade attached 97th Battery. " J.C. JOHNSTONE " " 368 " L.E. PAINTER returned from Gunnery Course at HAVERNAS to 10th Battery.	

1247 W 3299 200,000 (E) 8/14 J.B.C.&A. Forms/C. 2118/11.

Original   Army Form C. 2118.

Instructions regarding War Diaries and Intelligence
Summaries are contained in F. S. Regs., Part II.
and the Staff Manual respectively. Title pages
will be prepared in manuscript.

WAR DIARY
or
INTELLIGENCE SUMMARY
(Erase heading not required.)

Sheet 10

Hour, Date, Place	Summary of Events and Information	Remarks and references to Appendices
MAILLY MAILLET April 29th Contd.	A small party of the South Wales Borderers attempted to carry out a raid into the HAWTHORN REDOUBT at midnight. A large number of Batteries including 9.2" and 6" Hows, 60 pounders and Batteries of the RIGHT and LEFT GROUPS of the 29th Divisional Artillery took part both in the preliminary bombardment and later on to form a barrage. The raid was a failure on account of the raiding party starting 6 minutes before they should have and coming under fire from our own howitzers some of whom were shooting distinctly short. When our 33 casualties to a party of 70 are mainly on account of our own artillery promptly by a heavy bombardment of our own front and support trenches causing more casualties and a good deal of material damage. The 10th Battery participated and fired 396 rounds shrapnel and 132 rounds of H.E. during the operation. The 371st Battery withdrew from positions at BAIZIEUX AU BOIS and returned to AMPLIER.	

WAR DIARY
or
INTELLIGENCE SUMMARY

(Erase heading not required.)

Army Form C. 2118.

Sheet No. 11.

Hour, Date, Place	Summary of Events and Information	Remarks and references to Appendices
MAILLY MAILLET. April 30 15	Fine but overcast. Lieut HASKELL proceeded to HAVERNAS on gunnery course. CATTELL " " VALHEUREUX " benchmaker " 10 % battery did not fire — 37 1st — sent 2 officers and 54 O.R. to ENCLEBELMER to commence work on new position No 49932 Cpl. KINGTON E. 368th battery attached Y158 Trench Mortars 1676 Gnr KENNEDY.J.C.37th were wounded by enemy retaliation during the raid mentioned yesterday. Four Rifts were called in — Throughout the march great difficulty has been experienced in obtaining supplies of any description from Ordnance. There was a great scarcity of Telephone wire, all wire laid within 1500 yards of the front line has to form a metallic circuit to avoid risk of overhearing by the enemy this necessitated a double relay again down to the difficult nature of the country & are reg distant from Rear Railhead approximately 35 4 mile of wire.	B.S. Fowler Major R.G.A. Comdg 147

Confidential

MESSAGE.

***

FROM Lieut-General Sir Aylmer Hunter-Weston, K.C.B., D.S.O.

TO   All Officers and Men of the incomparable 29th Division, who took part with him in the historic landing on the Gallipoli Peninsula, 25th April, 1915.

On this, the first anniversary of the landing effected by the incomparable 29th Division near Cape Helles on the Gallipoli Peninsula, I send to each officer and man, who took part in that glorious operation of war, my personal greetings and congratulations on the privilege and opportunity which was accorded to you of being able to do so much for our beloved King and Country.

As fore-shadowed in the personal note I sent to each of you before we landed, you had to face death by bullet, by shell, by mine, by drowning. But nothing deterred either you that are here with me now, or those even more glorious comrades that have gone across the Great Divide and have attained the most noble end that can befall any man. It was your discipline, your training, and your fine esprit-de-corps that enabled you to carry on, notwithstanding your heavy losses, to stick it out, and to win through. You were successful in all the many engagements we fought together on the South end of the Peninsula, and the fact that our troops subsequently evacuated the Peninsula in no way dims the glory of your achievements. Indeed, the success of both the evacuations were greatly due to your good work.

In the great operations, which must come before this war is won by us, and in which we hope that it may be our good fortune to bear a leading part, I know that the 29th Division may always be relied on to emulate the noble example that it set itself a year ago today. This can only be if the officers and men, who have joined the Division in the past 12 months, determine that their discipline and spirit shall be of as high an order as that that enabled their predecessors to gain so glorious a place on the Roll of Fame.

I consider myself highly honoured to have the 29th Division under my command, and I look forward to taking part with it again in many a victorious fight.

       AYLMER HUNTER-WESTON.
         Lt-GENERAL.

Headquarters,
VIII Army Corps.
25th April, 1916.

29th Division.

147th BRIGADE

R. F. A.

MAY 1916

To D.A.G.
   3rd Echelon.

I beg to forward the original copy of the War Diary of 147th Brigade R.F.A. for the month of May 1916.

                    Lieut. Colonel.
        COMDG. 147th BDE. R.F.A.

147 Bde R.F.A. 29
Vol 3
N° I

Army Form C. 2118.

WAR DIARY
INTELLIGENCE SUMMARY
(Erase heading not required.)

Place	Date	Hour	Summary of Events and Information	Remarks and references to Appendices
MAILLY-MAILLET	MAY 1		Fine day – occasional "thunder showers": Lieut. Hart & 2nd Lt. Heath rejoined Brigade from Trench Mortar Battery (V/29) and went to their Batterys – 368th & 371st respectively.	
	2 3		Very fine day. Quiet on both sides. 10th Battery did not fire. Construction of 97 & r368th Battery positions pushed forward. The latter being almost complete but for head cover. Great difficulty experienced in getting material for same. Shortage of telephone wire continues. 31st Battery attached to Right Group – no position yet fixed for same. Cloudy, dull & close day. 104th Battery fired 46 rds. Shrapnel at 7 H.E. on HAWTHORN REDOUBT and Q10D100.80 – G11A0S.30. A barn fell at ENGLEBELMER, on 6 burrs of 371st Btry. and 4 of 97th Btry – killing one of the latter.	
	4			
	5 6 7		Dull & sultry day – wet night. 368th Battery drew some material for Battery position.
Dull day but much cooler – 10th " fired 44 rds. shrapnel & 10 H.E. on Q5D82.20 & Q12A0043.
Showery day. 368th Battery came up from AMPLIER and into action. Began line of same established at ACHEUX. 10th Battery fired 46 rds. shrapnel on Point – 77.00, 77.47 & 77.82 – Sgt H.E. DANIELS (31st Battery) and Dull but fine day, V/29 Trench Mortar Battery in action during night 7/8/6 –	
	8		Capt. F. Wilson (97th Battery) killed.	
	9 10 11		Fine & warm day. Very quiet on both sides – none of our Batterys fired.
Fine day – very foggy for observation purposes.
Very fine day, clear atmosphere – 10th Btry fired 39 rds. shrapnel on Q10D100.30 & point 7747. 368th Battery fired 6 rounds shrapnel on their datum point – Q5D70.40.	
	12		Dull and close day. 104th Bty fired 22 rds. shrapnel & 17 H.E. on point 7882. Q10D58.70. Q5D82.20 & between points – 7700 & 7747. 368th Btry fired 17 rds shrap. & 1 H.E. in registration of all four guns on Datum pt., also 1 round on enemy front line. Q10D58.30 – which fell short of our wire –	
	13		Very wet & dull day. Brigade Ammunition Column became N°3 Section Divisional Amm. Col. at 13.00. Construction of 97th Bty. position held up owing to shortage of material – principally timber. 368th Btry. fired 14 rds shrap. & 10 H.E. on re-registration of their datum point. 34 men & N.C.O's attached to 97th Btry. from D.A.C. to assist in construction of Battery position. Lieut Haskell returns from Hospital at OUEN – having apped his ankle while on Gunnery Course – posted to 371st Bty. with effect from today.	

1577 Wt.W10791/1773 500,000 1/15 D.D.&L. A.D.S.S./Forms/C. 2118.

Army Form C. 2118.

WAR DIARY
INTELLIGENCE SUMMARY (Cont'd)

(Erase heading not required.)

No. 11

Place	Date MAY	Hour	Summary of Events and Information	Remarks and references to Appendices
MAILLY-MAILLET.	14		Fine day, dull; Enemy fired 5-6 rounds (6.9") in close proximity to Bde. H.Q. (& Group H.Q.) killing 1 man - and a cow - in adjoining field - & causing slight damage to windows, walls, &c, of H.Q. Billet. Lt. R. McDonnelly rejoins Brigade from SIDI BISHR, EGYPT, + is re-posted to 97th Battery with effect from today. Lieut. Whatford and Strays join Brigade. The former posted to 4/5" Trench Mortar Battery & the latter to 10th Battery. 10th Bty fired 1 round on their Barrage line. (That manage-ment of "L" Bty). Gun emplacements, &c, falling in owing to want of maintenance of material for support pits & shells morning due wearing & very bright night. At 01.00 10th Bty. (under orders from Right Group) on Run Barrage line - during enemy bombardment on REDAN RIDGE. 368th Bty fired 6rds. Shrap. & 1 H.E. in registration of Y/9 4 gun on Q4.D95.50.	
	15		Fine day, very warm. Between hours 12.45-14.30 & 18.30-19.30 the enemy laid, in all, about 30 rounds (5.9") in close proximity to Bde gate (& Group) H.Q. about no of same falling within 70 yards of house - several as close as 2 or 3 yards. Some of the walls, windows & doors suffered today but otherwise little damage was done; A conference of left Group Battery Commanders was held when firing commenced between 18.30-19.30. Same adjourned to 15th M.A. Brigade H.Q. After the second round, which fell perilously close Col. Forman goes to see General Williams, he was killed for H.Q. - and gets one further seat in the town. 97th Bty. got some timber for gun position from wrecked houses at AUCHONVILLERS.	
	16		Lt. Pearson (10th Battery) proceeds on Artillery Course of Instruction to HAVERNAS. Very fine and warm day. Brigade H.Q. removed to new Billet (N°71) (which was vacated by M/7 Bty. R.F.A. which Battery being very close to the old H.Q. may have drawn the enemy's fire on to that zone.) 368th Bty. fired 22 rds. shrap. in registration of "L" Battery Barrage line.	
	17		Very fine & warm; 368th Battery takes over night & barrage lines of "L" Battery R.H.A. at 10.00. 10th Bty. fired 50 rounds between points 8583 - 4933. 368th Bty. fired 29 rds shrap. 2 H.E. - continued registration of "L" Battery lines. Also 8 rds shrap. 2 H.E. in retaliation to enemy's fire on left of our sector.	
	18		Very fine - clear atmosphere; 10th Bty fired 50 rds. shrap on wire cutting. 15 cm shell fell just short of 97th Bty. position. Still under construction. 368th Bty fired 2rd Shrap. 1 H.E. in registration of trenches Q17.8/22-90 in 36th Div. sector, for purpose of support lines.	
	19		Fine day. 368th Bty fired 9 rds shrap in registration of Barrage lines, with good effect. Quiet day.	
	20		Fine day; 368th Bty. fired 17 rds shrap. in registration. also 4 rds shrap. 2 H.E. in retaliation to enemy's fire. Owing to re-organization of 29th R.H.A. 371st Bty. 147th Brigade became 371st Battery, 132nd Bde. - being replaced by B/132 Bty. Vice 9/147. (4.5 How. Bty.)	
	21		Fine day. 10th Bty. fired 8 rounds H.E. for retaliation effect. 368th Bty. fired 10 rds shrap. 2 H.E.	
	22		Fine day. Enemy working party visit fired effect. Very quiet day on both sides. Lieut. Costello. R.F.A. - on round. 10 H.E. on their barrage lines.	
	23		Fine day. 10th Bty. fired 22 rds. shrap.	

WAR DIARY
INTELLIGENCE SUMMARY (Cont'd)

Army Form C. 2118.

Vol VIII

Place	Date	Hour	Summary of Events and Information	Remarks and references to Appendices
MAILLY-MAILLET	MAY 24		(97th Battery R.F.A.) posted to Brigade H.Q., as Orderly Officer to the Lt. Colonel commanding the Brigade with effect from today. 2nd Lieut G.G. Williams R.F.A. (Bde. H.Q.) posted to 97th Battery R.F.A. with effect from today. Fine and warm day: 368th Bty fired 19 rds T.S. & 10 H.E. on registration of enemy first line at Q.5.c.2.0.7.5. Normally quiet day.	
	25		Fine day. very warm. Chief target - Folk works 368th Bty. fired 9 rds T.S. + 7 H.E. on registering enemy front line immediately south of 88.69. also 10 rds H.E. in retaliation to enemy fire.	
	26		Fine day. Rather cool. Bombardment Bttty. 365th Bty fired 2 rds T.S. on return fire for purposes of calibration.	
	27		Dull day - cool. Bombardment still falling. very wet night. 368th Bty. fired 14 rds T.S. in registering & night firing for observation purposes. 368th Bty. fired 15 rds T.S. in registering "HAWTHORN REDOUBT".	
	28		Showery day - warm - rather cool. Barometer rising. 10th Battery changed from Gegam to ENGLEBELMER to MAILLY-MAILLETWOOD.	
	29		Fine day. rather warm - Barometer rising steadily. 10th Bty fired, not good effect, 19 rds T.S. + S.H.E. on enemy wire in front of R2.D.25.70.	
	30		Very fine. rather hot. atmosphere. Heat almost tropical. 368th Bty. fired 5 rds T.S. + 20 H.E. Very fine. Rather hot, damp atmosphere. 368th Bty. fired 14 rds T.S. in retaliation to enemy fire in registering enemy fire at Q.10. & 80.65. - also 14 rds T.S. in retaliation to enemy fire.	
	31		The Brigade Ammn. Column no longer exists as such.	

B.S. Morman
Lieut Colonel,
Comdg 147 Bde R.F.A.

29th Division.

147th BRIGADE

R. F. A.

JUNE 1916

SECRET

WAR DIARY

OF

147th BRIGADE RFA

FROM   JUNE 1st 1916

TO   JUNE 30th 1916

(VOLUME 10)

Appx T
Army Form C. 2118.

WAR DIARY
INTELLIGENCE SUMMARY
(Erase heading not required.)

Hour, Date, Place	Summary of Events and Information	Remarks and references to Appendices
June 1st 1916	Very fine day. 5 other ranks proceeded on leave to England. 10" Battery fired 38 rounds reporting thereafter, rates fires in road. D/147 obtained a registration on 'Y' Ravine by aeroplane observation. 368 Bty did not fire	
June 2nd "	3 other ranks 368 Battery proceeded on leave. 1 Gunner enemy wounded. Guns attacked to 97 Bty from 29 Div 368 Bty fired 7 rds to cover Trench Mortar Bty registration, also 28 rds registration of points on the front line. D/147 Bty fired 2 salvoes on BEAUMONT ROAD	
June 3rd	Fine. LOCKWOOD RSM T-30@ O/147 proceeded on leave. D/147 Bty continued their registration of Y Ravine by aeroplane observation and also fired by rates, on BEAUMONT ROAD. 10 Bty attempted to engage a hostile balloon but found at 368 Bty/@ Bty opp position Enemy 77 mm Bty	

WAR DIARY
or
INTELLIGENCE SUMMARY

Army Form C. 2118.

Sheet II

Hour, Date, Place	Summary of Events and Information	Remarks and references to Appendices
June 4th	368 Bty 70/147 took part in bombardment prior to raid by LANCASHIRE FUSILIERS at 12 mn last night on enemy front line trenches just N of HAWTHORN REDOUBT. Bombardment completely successful. Infantry got in front line un-opposed but found no men there. No prisoners were obtained. GOC 86th Inf Bde went round & complimented 10 Hy Bty & Arty units concerned. 10 Hy Bty fired 40 rds during the day registering the front line zones. The weather was much colder today.	
June 5th	10 Hy Bty 70/147 registered were hit the weather was very unsuitable for observation. 368 Bty did not fire. A draft of 13 Gunners + 7 OR arrived from the Base.	

WAR DIARY or INTELLIGENCE SUMMARY

Army Form C. 2118.

Sheet No

Hour, Date, Place	Summary of Events and Information	Remarks and references to Appendices
6th June	Very wet day. 368 Bty fired 4 rds on Station Point then the other Btys tried not fire. After dark the 97 Bty brought their gun into action at Q 16 c 30.15. Then Wagon lines n. with at AMPLIER.	
7th June	Another wet day. 97 Bty reported their Station Point ndoo STATION ROAD. 107 Bty fired 26 rds on wire.	
8th June	368 Bty reported that there were 4/147 Bty fired 6 rds on enemy trench mortar at Q.5c 30 no with good effect. Another very wet day. The trenches are in a deplorable condition.	

Army Form C. 2118.

Sheet IV

WAR DIARY
or
INTELLIGENCE SUMMARY

(Erase heading not required.)

Hour, Date, Place	Summary of Events and Information	Remarks and references to Appendices
9th June.	It rained lightly all day today. None of our Btys fired & the enemy was equally inactive	
10th June	10th Sty fired 22 rds registering the enemy support line. They had 1 man wounded 368 Sty registered 2nd line using 41/47 shrapnel. Enemy replied then front line was 4/47 Bty tried to get message to to retaliation. The Germans were everywhere reported being made during the night at THIEPVAL-	

Army Form C. 2118.

Sheet V

WAR DIARY
or
INTELLIGENCE SUMMARY

(Erase heading not required.)

Instructions regarding War Diaries and Intelligence Summaries are contained in F. S. Regs., Part II. and the Staff Manual respectively. Title pages will be prepared in manuscript.

Hour, Date, Place	Summary of Events and Information	Remarks and references to Appendices
11th June	Quite a fine day. 3 Telephones came from the Lines to the H.Q. 368 Bty fired 4 rds retaliation on Bde on Saxham Point. D/147 fired 6 rds on Trench Mortar at Q5C.40.35 + also fired 27 rounds retaliation.	
12th June	A fine day with occasional showers. 368" Bty reported parties of enemy support line 10"Bty fired 16 rds retaliation the enemy were exceptionally quiet to-day.	
13th June.	368 Battery fired on working parts in Q 110 with good effect.	

Army Form C. 2118.

Sheet VI

WAR DIARY
or
INTELLIGENCE SUMMARY
(Erase heading not required.)

Hour, Date, Place	Summary of Events and Information	Remarks and references to Appendices
14th June	A very quiet day. Strange and hard to observe the 875th fired SOS in retaliation. Lazy	
15th June	97 Sty fired 18 rds to find out the shortest range at which they could clear the crest. They discovered all the guns could be shortest to them. 368 Sty registered a different piece of front line wire at O.K.G. 0030. (pin) registered front line wire with SD rd. to Sty fired SO rds on short wire wire. A very clear day indeed.	
16th June	368 Sty fired 10 rds to let them entrain. Northern Switch + 20 rds registration of Station Road. Why fired 30HE registering front line. 10 Sty fired 16 rds on front wire.	

1247 W 3299 200,000 (E) 8/15 J.R.C. & A. Forms/C.2118/11.

WAR DIARY
or
INTELLIGENCE SUMMARY

(Erase heading not required.)

Army Form C. 2118.

Sheet VII

Hour, Date, Place	Summary of Events and Information	Remarks and references to Appendices
17th June	A fine day. 97 Bty fired 71 rounds wire cutting. 368 Bty fired 46 rds wire cutting. Bombarded this P.WIRE upon fwd Birds registering STATION ROAD. 10 Bty fired 68 rds registering PUISIEUX TRENCH + SUNKEN ROAD at R3c	
18th June	97 Bty fired 78 rds registration of BEAUMONT ROAD Ross & HERMAN & also reregistration of Barrage line. 368 Battery fired on enemy Machine Gun emplacement with good effect at m-7 reported Trench Mortar emplacement at Q10b-9280 + new aeroplanes on MAILY. MAILLET in evening Our batteries dropped shells on MAILY a flare when immediately Maily Station were packed with men and the Bn street perfect for observation 10 Bty wagon line parked for ENGLEBAMER WOOD to AMPLIER	

Army Form C. 2118.

WAR DIARY
or
INTELLIGENCE SUMMARY
(Erase heading not required.)

Sheet No.

Instructions regarding War Diaries and Intelligence Summaries are contained in F. S. Regs., Part II. and the Staff Manual respectively. Title pages will be prepared in manuscript.

Hour, Date, Place	Summary of Events and Information	Remarks and references to Appendices
19th June.	369 Sty fired 4 rds on HARBORO RAILWAY. D/147 Sty registered RAILWAY ALLEY. 10" Sty fired 76 rds on front line wire.	
20th June.	369 Sty registered the remainder of the wire which they have to cut. D/147 fired rds + 10" Sty 16 rds retaliation.	
21st June.	97 Sty fire 50 rds registration. 368 fired 15 rds retaliation. D/147 fired 11 rds registration of support trench to R.7b. 9 in the Wilhelm. 10" Sty fired 05 rds on Quarry in Q.12.b. The horse lines on the Rd. HdQrs were moved from MAILLY MAILLET to BAICHEUX.	

1247 W 3299 200,000 (E) 8/14 J.B.C. & A. Forms/C. 2118/11.

Army Form C. 2118.

Sheet IX

WAR DIARY
INTELLIGENCE SUMMARY
(Erase heading not required.)

Hour, Date, Place	Summary of Events and Information	Remarks and references to Appendices

22nd June.
The Lieut. Colonel Candy this day went to the new Lt. Group Hd Qrs in dugouts in the trenches MAILLY and ACHEUX MINERS. The Bde Hd Qrs now are in MAILLY. It was a very quiet day, our all Batteries reporting them were 368. Bty fired 3 ro. on Dakim Post. 10 Bty fired 15 ro. retaliation. A few shells fell in MAILLY in the evening, no cud. posts to Bde. DON'S Bty. 91 Bde communicated. All Batteries engaged in ammunition registration. Otherwise, guns for calibration. 9 Bty fired 70 to try new charge. No enemy aeroplane seen to be the last two nights. All Battery officers at coffee hour were recalled to the guns. Rev. J. Hunter.

23rd June
29 Dec Chaplain went to him with the 10" Battery HQ. Each Battery got 3 Joy Mortar Bombs. Energy big gun activity Thanks for Retrenchments.

WAR DIARY
or
INTELLIGENCE SUMMARY

Army Form C. 2118.

Sheet 10

Hour, Date, Place	Summary of Events and Information	Remarks and references to Appendices
24th June 1916 to 30 June 1916	Up to this date all Battns had been hard at work preparing for the bombardment of the enemy positions in neighbourhood of BEAUMONT HAMEL. The Bn was allotted to the 29 Divn Sector & was distributed into 2 Bns to right & left. The Right group was commanded by Lieut Colonel MORRMOUSE & Hq Dhu Bty were 15. D. 97. 20 (Catalogue Ran over Bde) H.Q. (117 Rds) + 370 SH(1000 Rds) The Left group was commanded by Lieut Colonel OF BROWN C in G 57 Bty Slip were 97 - 308 + D/mH (447 Rds) B. 2×4 Bty (15 - Rde B. H/m) r36a : D/ 33 (122 Rds) The telephone exchange at fact del Ore was exactly to all the Bty 6th park & the armies by wire formation groups on either flank & by cable laid in 6' deep trench. Those cable gave complete intelligence remained intact throughout the operations that slip had this been Believed for during not the OP had in trenches than what had not Refused us attempted. But them that had turn who arrayed was fighting that day of the armistice mag Suites out it was originally intended that there ought to 5 days of Preliminary bombardment beginning U to 7 June 24th Was Y day the tray Z 8 Bombardment commenced which on July 28	

Army Form C. 2118.

WAR DIARY
or
INTELLIGENCE SUMMARY
(Erase heading not required.)

Sheet 11.

Instructions regarding War Diaries and Intelligence Summaries are contained in F. S. Regs., Part II. and the Staff Manual respectively. Title pages will be prepared in manuscript.

Hour, Date, Place	Summary of Events and Information	Remarks and references to Appendices
24th June (cont) to 30th June.	On June 28th (Note X&Y) instructions were received that the day of the assault (one day) had been postponed 72 hrs. The days of bombardment were increased (Y, Z days) bringing the day of the assault to July 1st. The intellectual harassment of the enemy was continued to render the assault as bright as totally humiliating as possible. On a light railway running from ACHEUX to AVELUY VILLERS station they were frequently brought close to 1st our B.H.Q except J.J. Way had to buy up the [illegible] on their own account. The establishment of [illegible] were made [illegible] during the day. The B.H. requesting Convoy forwarding & [illegible] to B.H. requesting DHQ wagons waited afresh off the Btn, which was nightly the [illegible] of [illegible] the [illegible] after the bombardment. Congratulating the divine on their good work.	

1247 W 3299 200,000 (E) 8/14 J.B.C.&A.   Forms/C. 2118/11.

Army Form C. 2118.

WAR DIARY
or
INTELLIGENCE SUMMARY
(Erase heading not required.)

Sheet 12

Hour, Date, Place	Summary of Events and Information	Remarks and references to Appendices
24 June (cont) to 30th June	The rate duty 18 Prs during the preliminary bombardment was between 160 to 170 per gun per diem. 18 Prs Btys also participated in special concentrated bombardments at specified times each day. By night 2 guns of each Bty were on duty. By night about ? ? up a continuous fire on avenues of approach to the enemy front system. Each section fired 172 rounds nightly. The wire was successfully cut with along the front allotted. The 4.5 How cut did the same in conjunction with 60 Prs + each battery had in addition certain counterbattery trenches to deal systematically. Hy Arty fired at night along enemy communications.	

Army Form C. 2118.

Sheet 13.

WAR DIARY
or
INTELLIGENCE SUMMARY
(Erase heading not required.)

Instructions regarding War Diaries and Intelligence Summaries are contained in F. S. Regs., Part II. and the Staff Manual respectively. Title pages will be prepared in manuscript.

Hour, Date, Place	Summary of Events and Information	Remarks and references to Appendices
24th June 11th day	All Btys were engaged in cutting wire sweeping by night. The Step Bys on the right were attempting to subdue some good spots by night — there were two chapels round which through which 368 & 366 found no STATION. Red & green flares in BEAUMONT HAMEL by night. Infantry patrols did not get on as well. Rem Btys ran for fire on the TRENCHES & certain events of the area also took into con- sideration. Hostiles were rather deserted during the night.	
25th June V day	Same programme on v day. 368 Bty fired a great deal of percussion shrapnel burst to temple nests in their rests of phosphene. 3 hostile balloons brought down in flames by our aeroplanes. 3 other ranks Mrs Wt Cld. _____	
26th June W day	Special bombardmt 7am to 10:30am. 18 Trench Mortars bombard BEAUMONT HAMEL W cutting & trench patrol went out to see wire reports very satisfactory Smoke attack 10.15am X/y/29 & 6.15pm Enemy repd at 10.15am but only returned firing to facility attack. No guns used up to 5pm but put _____ of bursting shells _____ _____ fired, and — a fresh amount of _____ _____ _____ _____ in the _____	*Medium Trench Mortar Batty attd to the Sd

WAR DIARY
INTELLIGENCE SUMMARY
(Erase heading not required.)

Army Form C. 2118.

Hour, Date, Place	Summary of Events and Information	Remarks and references to Appendices
26th June (Cont)	Fire broke out RE dump near 447 M4 Oct & Military bunkball night Shock J/3 13 MARTIN R.H. 10 Sq R2a ported to 20 Divn Arty	
27th June Y day	Very wet day. Special bombardment to stop – 5 zero were cutting in wind. Dirty sky still a bit misty began in the afternoon with 200 field no casualties — the reinforcing guns came into position 4/29 inft a couple of hits mostly work No 2 gun 20 Rifle Grenades 9 men wounded	
28th June Y/day	Very wet bad light Special bombardment 5 am to 6.30 pm. J 9 - J.17 Hay were shelled with lachrymating shells. Hay got one gun into action but only got off a few rounds when rifle ammunition exploded with return of rifle ammunition — then had one blown in they were shelled at 2.30 pm Sections of smoke fired at 2.30 pm	
29th June Y day	Raid at 0100 Wycombe etc the front line was full of Huns free twice M2b - on pushed them out trying again J.13 D.14 G.3 fired 700 gas Front a TM attack – they did not come back were fired on by 4 machine guns in M.2b	2 other ranks D/100 Wounded

WAR DIARY

INTELLIGENCE SUMMARY

(Erase heading not required.)

Army Form C. 2118.

Sheet 15

Hour, Date, Place	Summary of Events and Information	Remarks and references to Appendices
30 June to day	that 3 of the steps have finished being wire cutting. Day spent in putting finishing touches to the safety on the new run. Nothing to report the first day. 1120 fires order when the reconnaissance Batt put down a by Bills the most of men sent back to ENGLEFMER burning a tram 81. 31 shot men Yeo gun which, with the Scouts in an hour's going over took 105 wounded. Initial plan brought down was GRANDCOURT by machine gun fire. Osho received but no reply to bear fife or to Trenche Wick on our left. Other Cantamolment to Philpotts Copse & Ksst Colony Rd. Coy 147 Sch Rifle.

29th Division.

147th BRIGADE

R. F F A.

JULY 1916

WAR DIARY

INTELLIGENCE SUMMARY

Army Form C. 2118

147 Bde R.F.A.

Part V

Instructions regarding War Diaries and Intelligence Summaries are contained in F.S. Regs., Part II. and the Staff Manual respectively. Title Pages will be prepared in manuscript.

Place	Date	Hour	Summary of Events and Information	Remarks and references to Appendices
In the field	1/7/16		**Z day** The infantry assault was timed to take place at 7.30 a.m. It was preceded by 65 minutes intense bombardment of the front line trenches by 18 pounders. All natures of artillery participated. Some of the Heavy Batteries commenced as early as 5 a.m. But it was obvious that no weight of heavy metal who on the enemy front line. A colossal mine under the HAWTHORN REDOUBT was sprung 10 minutes before 7.30. This turned out a fatal error. It gave away the show all along the line. It afforded an extra obstacle for our Infantry (the crater was 130 yards long), and being much nearer to the Huns than to ourselves it was promptly manned by them with machine guns. The result was that, except in isolated cases, the enemy front line was scarcely entered. The enemy front line trench had not actually been sufficiently damaged to prevent movement in rear of the dug-outs even before our 18 pounders lifted off the enemy front line. Many of the enemy machine guns were up on the parapet. Three other factors militated against the chances of success so far as our (29 Div) Infantry were concerned.	

Army Form C. 2118.

Sheet II

WAR DIARY
or
INTELLIGENCE SUMMARY
(Erase heading not required.)

Place	Date	Hour	Summary of Events and Information	Remarks and references to Appendices
	1/7/16.		Concerned: Heavy Artillery bombardment opened at 7.25 am – 5 minutes before Zero although this did not actually affect the enemy front line trench. It gave the occupants of the dug-outs a signal. (1) The breadth of No-man's land – never less than 200 yards – and our lift off the front line had to synchronise with the advance of our Infantry from our front line. Before our infantry could reach the enemy front line, they had then cut down by machine gun fire insufficiently cut from their dead. (2) Our own wire had been insufficiently cut. Our dead were down in twos & threes in the gaps therein. Our task on the 1st July (day of the assault) was to fire an intense bombardment on the enemy front line prior to the assault then to lift by increments of 100 yards at a time. We worked entirely by time table – as the infantry advanced. Each B.C. was no far as the troops was concerned in a copy of attached. Each B.C. made out a time-table for each of his guns worked independently as Battery or section fire out attached. Enf[?] emplacements to quite out of the question.	× forward to R.O. 3rd Div.

WAR DIARY or INTELLIGENCE SUMMARY

Army Form C.2118.
Sheet III

Place	Date	Hour	Summary of Events and Information	Remarks and references to Appendices
	1/7/16		Question. We did our allotted task, but as our infantry failed, except in isolated instances – to penetrate the enemy front line, our barrage ahead of the infantry represented so much ammunition wasted. As it was impossible, owing to the dust, smoke – difficulty of distinguishing from or he to stop unnecessarily our attack had failed. Thanks to our telephone lines in deep trenches the communications with the existing Group's worked excellently with the control of the 8 Batteries worked smoothly & harmoniously. Each Battery of the 147" Bde. supplied a Liaison Officer with an infantry Battalion on 1st July. Each Liaison Officer was accompanied by 2 telephonists. In spite of what the parties went through on that day – during the nights before & after, the officers went through unscathed – only 2 of the telephonists (both in 97 Battery) were wounded. Lieut. J.J.A. HART (368th) was attached to the 2nd R. Dublin Fusiliers. Lieut. W.C.E. ROBINSON (97th) to the 4" Worcesters. Lieut L.E. PAINTER (10th) to the 1st Borders and Lieut. F.G. LOCKWOOD to the 2nd Royal Fusiliers. The R.A. casualties was very slight – our gun positions being entirely left alone by the enemy. The only [to] be added was one within 300 yds of our front line this O.P. from fairly heavily shelled with 2 [...] [...] hostile aeroplanes [...] they were apparently [...] that a pin & group escape a S.9 [...] the bursts at the entrance to the O.P. – twenty yards [...]	

Army Form C.2118.

Sheet IV

WAR DIARY
or
INTELLIGENCE SUMMARY
(Erase heading not required.)

Instructions regarding War Diaries and Intelligence Summaries are contained in F. S. Regs., Part II. and the Staff Manual respectively. Title Pages will be prepared in manuscript.

Place	Date	Hour	Summary of Events and Information	Remarks and references to Appendices
	1/7/16		The guns answered well, the registrations for the barrage had been carefully carried out, there were no complaints from the Infantry. A good deal of the barrage shooting was entirely off the map owing to the configuration of the ground preventing close observation. The buffer springs of the guns were as usual the only sources of trouble. Owing to the rapid rate of fire and the wear to the circumstances of the day no note could be made of prematures. The enemy retaliated heavily on our front parties of trenches on our main communication trenches, completely blocking many of them. Our heavy Artillery — even 9.2 Howitzers — put many shots into our own trenches adding greatly to the horrors that our own Infantry had to undergo.	

WAR DIARY
or
INTELLIGENCE SUMMARY

(Erase heading not required.)

Army Form C. 2118.

Sheet Y

Place	Date	Hour	Summary of Events and Information	Remarks and references to Appendices
	1/7/16		The expenditure of ammunition was as under from 24th June, on which date each Battery had 1000 rounds per gun stored at the gun position. Each night from 24th/25th June, each battery received a convoy of 4 full wagons of ammunition (304 rounds) the Ammunition Column did wonderful work though the amount of opposition to certain Batteries (notably D/147) were constantly shelled there was never any delay never shortage of ammunition.	

Expenditure of Ammunition —

Date	10"				Total
24th June		478	368	21441	24445
25"		616	643	556	2755
26"		818	825	514	3247
27"		306	829	635	2511
28"		1524	815	599	4288
29"		499	1180	632	3084
30"		618	926	709	4152
			1621	841	
1st July		601	589	164	2495
		1141			

Grand Total for 6 a.m. on 24th June to 12 midnight 1st July 24897

Army Form C. 2118.

Sheet ii

WAR DIARY
or
INTELLIGENCE SUMMARY
(Erase heading not required.)

Instructions regarding War Diaries and Intelligence Summaries are contained in F. S. Regs., Part II. and the Staff Manual respectively. Title Pages will be prepared in manuscript.

Place	Date	Hour	Summary of Events and Information	Remarks and references to Appendices
	1/7/16		Another fine day. Arrangements were made for another attack to be delivered from the Right Sector. Some of our Batteries were to _____ in the bombardment but this was cancelled. Instructions were received that defensive tactics were to be adopted though considerable artillery activity was to be maintained by night & day. No one was to be kept open merely to deceive. Was to be made to annoy the enemy. The 368th Bty was ordered to fire on the HAWTHORN REDOUBT at 3.30 p.m. A special bombardment took place from 3 to 3.30 p.m. A Red X flag was seen flying when the Huns were seen coming out into No Mans Land. & crawl the trenches. About 10 p.m. this was reported that they were entering our _____ machine guns to the _____ . The wind was blowing the gas away. The Hun was getting the _____ (J.32.d) this gas was blowing back on our trenches. No casualties were reported 368th Bty had 19 rounds of active at night with grenades cartridge cases.	

2449 Wt. W14957/M90 750,000 1/16 J.B.C. & A. Forms/C.2118/12.

WAR DIARY
or
INTELLIGENCE SUMMARY

Army Form C. 2118.

Sheet VII

Place	Date	Hour	Summary of Events and Information	Remarks and references to Appendices
	3/7/16		MAILLY was heavily shelled in the afternoon. The 15 [Bde] went into tents in the orchards behind ENGLEBELMER. The 132 Bde H.Q. who had been in the same billet as the 147 Bde H.Q. also moved to ENGLEBELMER	
	4/7/16		Nothing to report. A very wet day	
	5/7/16		Very wet day with violent thunderstorm. After dark the 10th & 9th Battns. moved then Emm position back into position on outskirts of ENGLEBELMER. These positions which had been made by the French weren't very well protected from the 10" gun. 3am to 0AM7. 3am to NOYEUX 0/14. 3am in NOYEUX moved our wagon line to NOYEUX. Sent in rations horse line moved up the wagon line to the H.Qrs horse line was in	
	6/7/16		Nothing to report. Very wet day the trenches were in a very bad condition	

Army Form C. 2118.

WAR DIARY
or
INTELLIGENCE SUMMARY

(Erase heading not required.)

Sheet No. VIII.

Place	Date	Hour	Summary of Events and Information	Remarks and references to Appendices
	1/7/16		Another wet day. Special bombardment of enemy front line from 7.55 to 8.50 a.m. Usual light firing at intervals.	
	8/7/16		A fine day. Special bombardment from 7.55 to 8.30am. The Division bombarding a ridge front extending down to the River ANCRE. New OP's had to be selected & some registrated. New registration was required.	
	9/7/16		Fine all day. Special bombardment between 7.30 to 8.25 a.m during which smoke was liberated by us.	
	10/7/16		Nothing to report. A fine day	Hornet {day and night firing}
	11/7/16		Nothing to report. A fine day but cold	
	12/7/16		Nothing to report. A fine day	

Army Form C.2118.

Sheet IX

WAR DIARY
or
INTELLIGENCE SUMMARY
(Erase heading not required.)

Instructions regarding War Diaries and Intelligence Summaries are contained in F.S. Regs., Part II. and the Staff Manual respectively. Title Pages will be prepared in manuscript.

Place	Date	Hour	Summary of Events and Information	Remarks and references to Appendices
	13/7/16		Lieut. C.T. GRAY (10"Bty) took over command of D/132 Bty Rta. A raiding party went out at night attack at 12 mn after 2 hours bombardment but were unable to ride the enemy trenches. There was another bombardment from 2.30 to 3.30 am.	
	14/7/16		There were 3 bombardments to-day each of 9 minutes duration at 11.30 am, 2 pm, + 9 pm. Nothing else to report.	
	15/7/16		A Hun aeroplane dropped 2 or 3 bombs on MAILLY in the morning doing no damage. SUGAR FACTORY + COURCELETTE were seen to be blown up. 2nd Lieut W.H. CRAIG Rsn joined the 10 Bty today from England.	
	16/7/16		Very wet day. Lt Col Ra inspected the Bty Wagon lines to-day, the horses were looking fairly well considering the hard time they had during the winter desert trek. Weather cold + wet.	

Army Form C. 2118.

WAR DIARY or INTELLIGENCE SUMMARY
(Erase heading not required.)

Sheet X

Place	Date	Hour	Summary of Events and Information	Remarks and references to Appendices
	17/7/16		Lieut. C.S.S. MORGAN posted to 10 Bty. Rifle from No. 2 Sector. 2nd Div. Lieut. C.J. BRAVE was posted from the 10 Bty to No. 2 Station. Fine day all day — very quiet.	
	18/7/16		A draft of 8 telephonists arrived from the Base today but leaving but cleared up towards midday. The heat of Coy. went to see the ruins of FRICOURT today. the 368th Bty position was slightly shelled today. no casualties.	
	19/7/16		S.O.R. from the Bde went to Y.29 T.M. Bty today. This have had a good many casualties + also a great number of men going sick lately. 368th Bty took on a battle Bty another of POZIERES.	Y29
	20/7/16		Very hot day. Lieut K R Park went to hospital with fever. Lieut H MERRYWETHER (91 Bty) went out with patrol of Suffolks between our lines Two day shell H MERRYWETHER sent to arrest a small working party of the D.A.C. The divisional infantry are going to another front of the line the 25 Divn taking their places.	
	21/7/16		2nd Lieut M 25 Div Infantry Major LUSH-WILSON (10 Bty R.H.A.) was	

Army Form C. 2118.

WAR DIARY
or
INTELLIGENCE SUMMARY
(Erase heading not required.)

Sheet XI

Place	Date	Hour	Summary of Events and Information	Remarks and references to Appendices
	22/1/16		This day 20 or 30 gas shells were fired into MANCY WOOD in evening. NO casualties.	
	23/1/16		Lieut. Col. DE FORMAN R.F.A. who had commanded the Bde since 17th Oct 1915 was posted to command the 16 Bde R.H. Major M.R.F. COURAGE (370 Bty 152 Bde) took on command of the 147. Field accompanying the rank of Lieut-Colonel. Major H DENISON (3.8°) was offered the command of Y Bty R.H.A. but refused it. 19 Recruits arrived to the Bde last night. They were inspected by the G.O.C. R.A. the morning. They were a very good lot.	
	24/1/16		This day 2 Lieut G. GRIFFITH WILLIAMS (97 Bty) sent to hospital with fever. 2 Lieut W. J. NOWELL (Orderly Officer) posted to D/72 and 2 Lieut G. EAST (D/132) posted to Bde H.Q. to do duties as Orderly Officer.	
	25/1/16		This day a Conference of Bde Commanders. There are try groups establishedby the Bdys are to be divided up as follows the EAST Centre & left to be but to the Centre group & Right with the Right Sect O.P. at Old Shellyrates, 13, 26, 92, 10", +60"(D/17). Central group (14 Bde - Lt Col. Smith), 369, 310, 371, 368, D/132. Left group (15 Bde - Lt Col Forman.) (a + b) Y, 97, D/147.	

Capt A.H.T. HYSLOPP the Vet officer a great great work with the veterinary work after this transport demands

Army Form C.2118.

Sheet XII

WAR DIARY or INTELLIGENCE SUMMARY
(Erase heading not required.)

Place	Date	Hour	Summary of Events and Information	Remarks and references to Appendices
	20/7/16		This day the 147 Field Heavy artry were Rest of 6 ENGLEBELMER, vacated by 17 Fde HQ. The horses were brought up to the new position for ACHEUX. Lieut E F COSTELLO who had been doing Staff Officer for the left group returned to the 97th Bty today. Lieut G EAST in accordance with the Centre group, to look after the telephones. A few 7 cm shells fell in neighbourhood of 97 Bty in the evening a 5.9 shell fell into the 368 Bty Cook house burying the 2 cooks — they were dug out unharmed.	
	21/7/16		Another fine day. Lieut H MEREWETHER (97 Bty) returns from the WAC. All our Battery lines ordered to move to BERTRANCOURT. 29 D.A. H.Q. was now for ACHEUX to BERTRANCOURT. 5/147 Bty was heavily shelled with gas near dusk about 1030 pm. One man was sent to hospital next day. The remained his g^{as} helmet too soon finding it very stuffy. no other casualties.	

WAR DIARY or INTELLIGENCE SUMMARY

Army Form C. 2118.

Sheet XIII

Place	Date	Hour	Summary of Events and Information	Remarks and references to Appendices
	28/7/16		Beautiful day. 2 aeroplanes were sent from HQrs Staff to assist Right Group. All our Rly Wagn have been ordered to move to another part of the line. BERTRANCOURT was expended dangerous owing to the open before this was excavated. They are to die increasing activity of enemy aeroplanes. Another 5.9 landed in the 368th dummy wreath at last. Another Cook House which is now empty 2 HQrs Officers Mess. Cook House which is now empty 2 enemy aeroplane came over an hour in the evening.	
	29/7/16		Very hot indeed. The Reat. Col Candy Rode round the ruins of LA BOISELLE today.	
	30/7/16		Another hot day. The Reut Colonel Candy inspected all the Battery wagons here in marching Order. There has been a very noticeable improvement in the condition of the horses in the last week. The Gunners were jolly glad to fall in good order the there clothing was mostly gone but there is a good deal of personal equipment still deficient.	

H. C. Twiss Lieut Colonel
Commdg. 107 Bde R.F.A.

29th Division.
----666-

147th BRIGADE

R. F. A.

AUGUST 1 9 1 6

WAR DIARY or INTELLIGENCE SUMMARY

147th Bde R.F.A. Army Form C. 2118.

Shut I

Vol 6

Place	Date	Hour	Summary of Events and Information	Remarks and references to Appendices
	1/8/16		A fine day. 4 hostile aeroplanes came our lines towards evening — the first seen for over a week. 368th Bty was shelled at night. 1 Direct hit on one gun emplacement also direct hit on one officers dugout. No casualties.	
	2/8/16		Fine day. The OC Bde takes over command of the left group vice Col Forman who went to hospital with a strained cartilege. The 15th Bde HQ continue to "run" the left group. 10th Bty move into new position in MESNIL VALLEY next door to then old position the telephone exchange.	
	3/8/16		The wagon lines are very busy at present having to bring up 600 rnd. rpd. a day. The horses are not looking too well. Lieut. F.O.BAIN, Lieut. R.C.DONNOLLY & Lieut. A.F.LEIGHTON promoted full Lieutenant (undated). 1 man of the Hd Qrs accidentally wounded in the foot.	
	4/8/16		2nd Lieut K R PARK returns from hospital. Cold windy day. 10th Bty shelled with 77 mm Wagon lines are going to be shifted back to ACHEUX.	
	5/8/16		Cloudy & cold. Orders come in that wagon lines will move to LOUVEN COURT (not ACHEUX) on 7th inst.	

WAR DIARY or INTELLIGENCE SUMMARY

Army Form C. 2118.
Sheet 2

(Erase heading not required.)

Place	Date	Hour	Summary of Events and Information	Remarks and references to Appendices
	6/8/16		Fine day. D/147 Shelled with 8" H.V. not in all N.W. echelsti. Hostile aeroplane was photoing; the railway line was but in 3 places.	
	7/8/16 8/8/16 9/8/16		All the Bty wagon lines move to LOUVENCOURT. 97" Bty Shelled - no casualties to personnel or equipment 5 men. D/147 Bty wounded by premature (?) from own gun. Shield gave no protection. Lieut CRAIG's 70 volunteers for French Mortars to report to V/29. 97" Bty move back to their old position at MESNIL VALLEY.	
	10/8/16 11/8/16		Rained all day. Nothing to report. Col. COURAGE Chig. back to Isle H.Qrs. He "29"DA being reorganised into 2 Groups. Major H DENISON (36") Sgn. 6"DHA" relieve Jno. A'rat being run down at invitation of GOC RA DA.	
	12/8/16		Fine day. Lieut G. GRIFFITH WILLIAMS from back to his hospital to posted to 10"Sty. No Sgt SMITH (10"Sty) gassed + sent to hospital.	
	13/8/16		A great number of gas shells fell in MESNIL VALLEY at night. 10"Sty heavily shelled. Captain I.M.H.C. BATTEN wounded + sent to hospital, also Sgt & 1 BSM. 1 gun knocked out.	

War Diary or Intelligence Summary

Army Form C. 2118. Sheet 3

Date	Summary of Events and Information
14/8/16	Very wet day. Major DENISON returns from 29 DAHQ where he went for a "rest cure". Lieut. R.C. DONNOLLY (97" Bty) takes over temp. command of 10" Bty. 1 section 10" Bty more trek to their old position in MABOTH'S vineyard on the outskirts of ENGLEBELMER. They could not move out until 3 am on morning of 15" as the MESNIL VALLEY was bombarded with gas shells. 2 gun 368" Bty out of action with broken springs. The O.C. Bde inspected the wagon lines at LOUVENCOURT.
15/8/16	The D.A.C. are going to bring up ammn. for Btys from today to give our horses a much needed rest. The other section 10" Bty now trek to MABOTH'S Vineyard & the whole of 97" Bty now trek to old position of at ENGLEBELMER. Very wet all day.
16/8/16	Fine day. 29 Da reorganised into 3 Groups again. 147 In Bde HQ take over left group. There down to left groups dugouts — the horses remaining on the hill. Btys of left group are B, L, Y, 97" & 460. 10" & D/147" are in the Right group — 368" Bty in Centre Group.
17/8/16	Fine day. Nothing to report.
18/8/16	Wet day. 13" Bty (situated between left group & centre left group dugouts) were shelled with 5.9" & 8" forced to evacuate their position. Only 3 men wounded.

WAR DIARY
or
INTELLIGENCE SUMMARY

(Erase heading not required.)

Army Form C. 2118.

Sheet 4

Place	Date	Hour	Summary of Events and Information	Remarks and references to Appendices
	19/8/16		Nothing to report	
	20/8/16		Fine day. Hostile Arty very active. "A" Bty were shelled with 4.2.0's 75's 9c's but withdrew their detachments with only 1 man wounded. Hostile aircraft more active.	
	21/8/16		Fine day. 10th Bty shelled with 5.9's - no casualties. Raid made by us in Centre Redt. a failure.	
	22/8/16		Fine day. Raid in left sector cancelled	
	23/8/16		Fine day. Nothing to report	
	24/8/16		Captain C.H. CALVERT (2g Da H.O.) TMO posted to take over command of 10th Bty RFA. Lieut R.C. DONNOLLY reports 97th Bty. Lieut E. J. COSTELLO (97th Bty) posted to 10th Bty. Lieut G. GRIFFITH. WILLIAMS (10 Bty) posted to 97 Bty.	
	25/8/16		This morning but followed by rain in the afternoon. Colonel inspected how it Major Lewis B at L Battries in the Brigade. He considers them in excellent condition and that 8th & 89th Bty L Battn RFA was especially noticeable, but he knows generally shown a lack of condition, probable due to the early work and muddy standings. there resulting from the recent rain. Capt. Lt A. J. Leighton takes over the port L Adjutant vice 2 Lt A.M. MacEachen to the 368th Battn RFA.	

WAR DIARY
or
INTELLIGENCE SUMMARY

Army Form C. 2118.
Sheet 5.

Place	Date	Hour	Summary of Events and Information	Remarks and references to Appendices
	25/8/16		3 Sergts. 3 Bombardiers joined from the Base. 15 others (5 riding, 10 light draught) also joined from Remount Depot.	
	26/8/16		A normal day. During the night 97th Battery RFA moved into their forward position in the Mesnil Valley. 2/Lt K L M K Pierson admitted to hospital.	
	27/8/16		Weather very unsettled - very little sunshine and heavy showers. 97th Battery RFA established in their new position - their old position being occupied by a Battery of the incoming division. Orders issued to begin wire cuttings on the new position for the front allotted to this Brigade. During the night the 10th Battery RFA moved up to their old forward position in the Mesnil Valley. The operation was much hampered by rain, but the move was carried out in a satisfactory manner.	
	28/8/16		Weather still thoroughly unsettled and heavy showers experienced throughout the day. Lt. Col. M R Enough took over the command of the Regt Front and Colonel Lott left for eighteen go took him to assist in digital operations in the latter Front. 10th Battery RFA established in their new position.	
	29/8/16		A heavy thunderstorm at mid-day followed by some rain later. The weather during the last few days had been so bad, that both roads and tracks were in a very muddy condition; and in consequence impending operations considerably delayed. Bombardment by Heavy Howitzers in the morning, and much good work done in aircraft, which were employed in very great activity on the day.	

WAR DIARY
or
INTELLIGENCE SUMMARY

Army Form C. 2118.

Sheet 6.

Place	Date	Hour	Summary of Events and Information	Remarks and references to Appendices
	29/5/16		B the German Anti-Aircraft Guns. Thus far the continued, but has not inflicted the broken the keenness observation. One of our aeroplanes was brought down by a hostile plane, which accounted for the occupants not having gunfire and our plane descended near Knightsbridge Barrack.	
	30/5/16		Very wet weather, which further impeded operations. This has and is for the preceding days has entering had been in progress. Germans in Ablois with their Artillery on our lines of communication and villages. The they carried out at short intervals during the day and night by a concentration of large and small guns, which fired at the rate of roughly twenty four rounds to minute - guns a few hours on their part and it caused considerable damage. Mailly, Jouaville, Fauboults were included in their bombardment. Observation posts were also heavily shelled throughout the day. The Capt. Colbert had a lucky escape from being buried in a dug-out.	
	31/5/16		A fine sunny day, in complete contrast to the weather of the preceding days, but not sufficient to dry up the trenches and roads which by now were in very bad condition. Intervals without bombardment carried out by an enemy the day. During the night a large number of gas shell were fired by the Germans, but caused no apparent damage. The latter was in conjunction with their short bursts of violent fire, which still continues on our lines of communication and villages.	

29th Division.

147th BRIGADE

R. F. A.

SEPTEMBER 1916

CONFIDENTIAL

WAR DIARY

OF

147th BRIGADE RFA

FROM 1/9/16 TO 30/9/16

(VOLUME 12)

Army Form C. 2118.

WAR DIARY or INTELLIGENCE SUMMARY

Sheet I.

(Erase heading not required.)

Instructions regarding War Diaries and Intelligence Summaries are contained in F. S. Regs., Part II. and the Staff Manual respectively. Title Pages will be prepared in manuscript.

Place	Date	Hour	Summary of Events and Information	Remarks and references to Appendices
MAILLY MAILLET FRANCE.	1/9/16		Nothing of importance occurred. The usual bursts of fire on MAILLY-MAILLET took place at odd intervals during the day and night. Operations had been delayed owing to rain, but the weather of these two days had dried the ground considerably. The necessary preliminary preparations were made for the attack in the morning.	
"	2/9/16			
	3/9/16		For the dawn of the attack from length, at 0.5 b. the rivers ANCRE. Artillery of 29th Division here covering this sector and divided into two Groups. The Right Group under the Command of Lt. Col. M.R.J. Conway. The left under Lt. Col. Marriott-Smith D.S.O. B Lt. 10- 11th Battery were attacked to the former and 365th Bty, 97th Bty, and D/147 Bty to the latter. The Director was the German third line opposite the sector. Description and account written by Lt. Col. M.R.J. Conway is as follows.	
		0.3.45	Group O.P. and all Battn. O.P.'s manned and communication satisfactorily established	
		0510- 0601	Bombardment carried out as per programme and worked very well.	
		06.03	D/132. (4.5 How.) was turned on to Counter-Attack lines at rate B 1 rd. per gun per min.	
		06.05	At request of O.C. 11th Sussex Regt. all 18pdr. Batteries brought back to reserve lines kept there at 4 rds. per gun per min. for 11 mins.	
		06.16	All 18pdr Batteries brought back to Support line Target at same rate for 14 mins.	
		06.30	All 15 howr Batteries lifted to Reserve line for 30 mins. as there parrage was asked for by G.O.C. 116. Infantry Brigade	
		07.00	Rate of fire reduced to 2 rds. per gun per min.	
		07.10	Rate reduced to 1 rd. per gun per min. Situation now rather obscure. Two red flares were observed at 07.20 in German support line in left front of 11th Sussex Batt.	

Army Form C. 2118.

WAR DIARY
or
INTELLIGENCE SUMMARY.
(Erase heading not required.)

Sheet 3.

Place	Date	Hour	Summary of Events and Information	Remarks and references to Appendices
	3/9/16		From personal observation and what afterwards received from our own Infantry, the line appears to have been insufficiently cut and where Officers no obstacle to an advance. The casualties in the Hans. Land at the first advance were very small. The first wave went over at time without any difficulty, but the second was afterwards, being one at the start and was late. The German Barrage was slow in starting, but getting much effect till 05.30, and some Bn. shooting appeared at first to be very wild. Then afterwards shelled our first line system rather heavily. Our Barrage was reported to be perfectly satisfactory and our Infantry advanced up to it well, but it would have suited them better if it had been kept on the support line for a larger period. The infantry not being able to advance sufficiently fast, why one machine gun was found in no Zone and the gunners were seen still alive. The trenches were very much knocked about and in many places they could not pass along without showing themselves. The failure to hold the position gained seems to have been caused by not sufficient Infantry getting over and inability to deal with the Enemy. They did find sufficient Infantry reported that the Germans came up through the C.T. Tunnels and got behind our Infantry, heavy parties of them could be observed in different places by the first line after our Infantry had got into their support trenches. So in places our Infantry were being fired in at our men rounded and otherwise in No Mans Land, and the Artillery of 39th Div. in whose sector they were turned on them. Communication — I was in Communication in all lines for all the period except for a short time when the line running both O.P. was cut by Shell. I obtained most useful information from the O.C. 115 Brigade, who knew its position with Lt. Col. Bletson the senior Officer, and was also in constant communication with the O.C. 116th Bgde, and my alterations in programme were carried out in collaboration with them. I also obtained much useful intelligence from the O.C. Battn in the front, who carried out the programme by left, and all subsequent operations with great promptitude. G.O.C. 116 Infantry Bgde informed me that he and all his officers were well pleased with the efficiency of the Barrage	

WAR DIARY
INTELLIGENCE SUMMARY

Army Form C. 2118.
Sheet 4.

Place	Date	Hour	Summary of Events and Information	Remarks and references to Appendices
France	3/9/16		and the effects [ ] fire. There were no casualties to men or equipment during the operations. "B" Battalion.	
	4/9/16		A quiet day. Nothing of interest occurred. Information arrived that both in two days the Division would move North to join the Infantry at Ypres.	
	5/9/16		During morning Brigade Headquarters was moved from Left Group H.Q. to Wagon Lines on hill situated on road to FORCEVILLE. Night Firing set. 7 drivers and 3 gunners joined from the Base. 97th Bty, 10th Bty, and 1 section each of 368th Bty and D/147 Bty, were withdrawn from the line, having been relieved by Batteries of the 39th Division. They proceeded to LOUVENCOURT, where they passed the night with their wagon lines.	
	6/9/16		Very fine day. Remaining sections of 368th Bty and D/147 Bty, withdrawn from the line, whence they joined the remaining portions of their Batteries at their wagon lines at LOUVENCOURT, where they remained during the day and that night. The Brigade Headquarters Staff under Command of Lt. Col. M.R. Y Cowap, R.F.A., the 10th and 97th Batteries, marched independently to FAMECHON, having through LOUVENCOURT, VAUCHELLES, THIÈVRES, and arriving at FAMECHON about 3. P.M. 2Lt. W.C.E. Robinson 97th Bty. R.F.A. has proceeded sick to Hospital.	

Army Form C. 2118.

WAR DIARY
or
INTELLIGENCE SUMMARY.
(Erase heading not required.)

Sheet. 5.

Instructions regarding War Diaries and Intelligence Summaries are contained in F.S. Regs., Part II. and the Staff Manual respectively. Title pages will be prepared in manuscript.

Place	Date	Hour	Summary of Events and Information	Remarks and references to Appendices
France	7/9/16		Brigade H.Q. Staff. Hear, 16th Bde., 97th Bde. Leave FAMECHON and marching through AMPLIER, DOULENS, march to HEM. Hear to be joined by 368th Bde. and D/147 Battery, which marched independently from LOUVENCOURT. 12 Riding horses and 6 light draught were allotted to the Brigade and were distributed during the course of the afternoon. Weather still being fine.	
	8/9/16	9. A.M.	Brigade, now joined up and under Brigade arrangements continued the march, passing thro' OCCOCHES, MÉZEROLLES, FROHEN-LE-GRAND, VILLERS L'HÔPITAL, FORTEL, CONCHY-SUR-CANCHE to EPS MONCHEL.	
	9/9/16	8.30 A.M.	Weather continued fine and sunny. Brigade's marching through BLANGERVAL, LINZEUX, OEUF, BEAUVOIS, PERREMONT, FLEURY, ANVIN to EPS. Just N.N. of LINZEUX the C.R.A. Brig.- General Malcolm Peake 29th D.A. inspected the Brigade, as it marched passed.— No compliments were given.	
		7. P.M.	Lt Col M.R.F. Courage R.F.A. lectured to the Officers in "Mared Discipline".	
	10/9/16	9. A.M.	Weather still fine and the road in good condition. Brigade marching through FIEFS, FEBVIN, PALLART, FLECHIN, CUHEM, ENQUIN-LES-MINES, ENQUINEGATTE, to THÉROUANNE.	
	11/9/16	10. A.M.	Fine. Brigade marching through CLARQUES, WARDRÊQUES, STATION, EBBLINGHEM, CHAT. LE NIEPPE, L'HEY, LEMENEGAT, to ARNEKE.	

Army Form C. 2118.

WAR DIARY
INTELLIGENCE SUMMARY.
(Erase heading not required.)

SHEET 6.

Place	Date	Hour	Summary of Events and Information	Remarks and references to Appendices
France	18/9/16		From 6 A.M. the re-organisation of this Brigade Completed. The Division now consists of 3 Brigades - 15th Brigade with 3 18 pdr Batteries, 1 4.5 How. 17th Brigade with 3 18 pdr Batteries, 1 4.5 How. and 147th Brigade with 2 18 pdr Batteries and 1 4.5 How To effect the latter, the 368th Battery was disbanded to make 6 gun Batteries of the 10th and 97th Bty. The Left Section with 1st Section Commander 2Lt. K.R. Park joined the 10th Bty., and the Right Section with 1st Section Commander Lt. J.A. Hart joined the 97th Bty. Major Brown D.S.O. R.F.A. Commanding the former, and Capt. K.M. Ball R.F.A. (with Capt. Calvert R.F.A. second in command) the latter, with Lt. A.M. McEacken second in command. 2 Lt. J.C. Johnstone, the remaining subaltern of the 368th Battery was attached to the 10th Bty. Stores and Transport which until disposed of, were divided up between the two Batteries concerned. D/147 Battery R.F.A. remained as the Howitzer Battery of the Brigade.	
		10. A.M	97th Battery joined up in conjunction with its new section, marched independently to its Wagon Line position near POPERINGHE.	
		11.00	Remainder of Brigade marched to their wagon lines via LEDRINGHEM, WORMHOUDT, HERZEEL & HOUTKERQUE. remainder of the day spent in making necessary arrangements in the new lines lines. One small shower fell during the morning, but this was the only rain experienced on the march, which had ideal weather throughout.	

Army Form C. 2118.

WAR DIARY
or
INTELLIGENCE SUMMARY

Sheet 7.

(Erase heading not required.)

Hour, Date, Place	Summary of Events and Information	Remarks and references to Appendices
France	**Comments on March.**	
	The March took place in Ideal weather and the Condition of Men + Horses improved every day — The Horses of the Brigade had mostly suffered from the effects of overwork during operations from July 1st onwards & had never properly recovered but they got better as the march went on without any casualties — The men were observing plenty to get on the move again & their behaviour was very good — The march throughout was good —	
13/9/16	This the Colder Day spent in establishing arrangements for magazines.	
14/9/16	Similar to 13/9/16	
15/9/16	Orders received that in the morning the Brigade was to take over that portion of the line then occupied by the 93rd Bgde R.F.A. 4th D.A. and relieve the latter. The Colonel, Adver. Officer and Brigade Signaller & 2 Officers from each Battn both Officer signallers proceeded to YPRES in order to inspect Gun Positions OP's and line system. The Antgaic Brigade the following Officers were similarly taken to the Re-organization and were dispatched as follows:— H.Q. Staff attached to No.3 Sec. D.A.C. 2Lt. G.B. East from 10th Bty R.F.A. — No.3 Sec. D.A.C. 2Lt. C.S.S. Morgan 10th Bty R.F.A. — No.4 Sec. D.A.C. 2Lt. J.C. Johnstone 10th Bty R.F.A.	

WAR DIARY or INTELLIGENCE SUMMARY

Army Form C. 2118.
Sheet 8.

(Erase heading not required.)

Hour, Date, Place	Summary of Events and Information	Remarks and references to Appendices
Belgium. 15/9/16	2 Lt. J.C. Johnston's health not allowing him to proceed to the D.A.C, to remain for the time being attached to the 10th Bty. R.F.A. 2 Lt. H.B. Thompson 132 Bde H.Q posted as Orderly Officer to 147th Bde H.Q.	
16/9/16 10.A.M	Headquarters wagon lines moved into vicinity of POPERINGHE adjoining that of the 92nd Bty. R.F.A. During the morning, the Colonel and Officer of the Brigade, gunners and signallers moved out to their respective positions. The 26th, 92nd & D/17 Batteries were attached to this Brigade, which will henceforward form Left Front under the Command of Lt. Col. M.F.J. Carnegy R.F.A. The 17th Bde H.Q being to reserve at HOUTKERQUE walks where they took on the wagon lines of this Brigade. Since 2 Lt. H.B. Thompson was proceeding on leave the following day, 2 Lt. T.C. Ralston 17th Bde R.F.A took over the duties of Orderly Officer and was temporarily attached to the Brigade.	
6.P.M	Wire taken over by from 93 Bde R.F.A & H.D.A. The front being Ref. 27 Julien Map C.22b 60.00 — C.29 d.45.40. Weather uncertain. Front quiet - a few rounds fired in re-registration and retaliation.	
17/9/16	Heavy shower. Leave to Shorest with a view to giving leave to Officers in turn. Who had not had leave for the last year. 6.15 to 6.45 Haymarket heavily shelled by the Germans. The day otherwise normal.	
18/9/16		

Army Form C. 2118.

WAR DIARY
or
INTELLIGENCE SUMMARY   Sheet 9

(Erase heading not required.)

Instructions regarding War Diaries and Intelligence Summaries are contained in F.S. Regs., Part II. and the Staff Manual respectively. Title pages will be prepared in manuscript.

Hour, Date, Place	Summary of Events and Information	Remarks and references to Appendices
20/9/16 0200 Belgium	Raid attempted. Place to be raided was at Map St Jean C.29.d. 40.15. The enemy wire was to have been cut by Bangalore Torpedo and the flanks on either side of the cutting managed by the 18th battn. B/Mn Brigade with the addition of the 26th and 92nd Batteries, 17th Brigade D/147 and D/117 the 4.5 How. Batteries B/Mn Front were allotted special parts in the shoot to form a barrier between 2 known Batteries also participated. The Raiding Party met a hostile patrol in front of the enemy wire, and was unable to effect a passage through. The latter with the Bangalore Torpedoes in again
Access to the trench at 0200 as per programme. The heavy trench artillery opened fire and continued till 0230. at various rates of fire. As far as could be ascertained the fire effect was good but since the raid itself had failed, little information could be gleaned on this point. 18 Pdr Batteries fired 768 rds, 4.5 Hrs. 134 rds and 6" How. 45 rds respectively. The Siemen Officers little retaliation and everything was generally quiet for the remainder of the day, which has inclined to be wet and stormy.	
21/9/16 22/9/16 23/9/16 24/9/16	General. Quiet and without Importance occurred. A certain number of rounds fired in registration and retaliation.	

WAR DIARY
or
INTELLIGENCE SUMMARY

(Erase heading not required.)

Army Form C. 2118.

Sheet 10.

Hour, Date, Place	Summary of Events and Information	Remarks and references to Appendices
25/9/16	A normal day. Usual number Grenades fired in return. Registrations and also for Retaliation 2Lt L.E. Lothian. Points 10 & 13 to R.F.A. transferred from the Brigade and posted to 4th Divisional Artillery.	
26/9/16 27/9/16 28/9/16	Normal days. Both Battery Registrations occuring at 28th 2W.E. Bang. D/147 Bty. had to send forward 38th Divisional Artillery Battery had also a Steam amount of practice in Co-operation with aircraft.	
29/9/16	A considerable number of rounds fired by the Howitzer B registration points of Gueudecourt and Sars Abraham were kept through the afternoon. Subsequent observation showed damage to Trench Mortars. A Lewis retaliation was organised, and the Kenot Muta. Subsequently silenced. During the night a few hundred rounds were fired in support of the 38th Divisional Artillery, who have been carrying out a raid in conjunction with the Infantry. The raid however not a success, due to the fact that no enemy was found in the advanced positions raided, and no identification were obtained.	

WAR DIARY
or
INTELLIGENCE SUMMARY

Army Form C. 2118.

Sheet II.

Hour, Date, Place	Summary of Events and Information	Remarks and references to Appendices
30/9/16	Fine. Day normal, but a few rounds fired to register special points for the raid.	
	The Raid	
	Successfully carried out. The absence of short bursts and prematures was most noticeable. The raid was carried out by 30 men and an Officer of the 1st Border Regiment who were assisted by a violent bombardment on its line chief opposite WIELTJE. (It is understood Maj. St Jean C. 29 a 30 9 5) About 5000 shots altogether fired in the centre in the space of an hour.	
20.15.	All guns and Trench Mortars on the outpost in Right Zone kept up a 10 minute cannonade, to which the enemy replied with Minenwerfer and several Salvoes from Field Guns.	
20.30	The Bombardment Commenced and was unaccompanied by any retaliation from Hostile Batteries which put up a half-hearted Barrage. When he ceased fire and the troops had safely returned. His fire lasted for 35 mins. and was directed on our front line. Report by 1st Robinson 1st Border Reg! Officer in charge of raid :- Artillery Preparation most successful. (a) bone cut (b) no short shell. (c) no short bursts and Enemy shown to dug-outs by intensity Bombardment. Trenches front line system torn very slightly damaged. Men and several unburied bodies. The Raiders got safely back with 12 prisoners no one so far been wounded (slightly) by enemy rifle fire machine guns were silenced by our shell fire, but control officers were seen diving to the Artillery Preparation. Lt. Robinson said the great assistance that enabled Raiders to achieve results without molestation was the Artillery preparation.	

29th Division.

147th BRIGADE

R. F. A.

OCTOBER 1916

SECRET

WAR DIARY

147th BRIGADE RFA

FROM OCT 1st 1916

TO OCT 31st 1916

(VOLUME 14)

Army Form C. 2118.

WAR DIARY
or
INTELLIGENCE SUMMARY SHEET 1
(Erase heading not required.)

Instructions regarding War Diaries and Intelligence Summaries are contained in F. S. Regs., Part II. and the Staff Manual respectively. Title pages will be prepared in manuscript.

Hour, Date, Place	Summary of Events and Information	Remarks and references to Appendices
YPRES 1/10/16	Fine. A quiet day with a few rounds fired in Retaliation	
2/10/16 3/10/16 4/10/16	normal days weather generally fine but dull	
5/10/16 6/10/16 7/10/16	Fine - Infantry of 29th Div. relieved by Infantry of 55th Div. Relief carried out satisfactorily and quietly. Weather fine but little sunshine - normal days except for increased Trench Mortar Activity by the enemy, against whom retaliation was given in each instance.	
8/10/16	In view of the relief of the Brigade by the 277th Bgde RFA 55th D.A., the Battery positions, O.P's, Wagon Lines and Bgde. H.Q's were visited by Advanced Parties of the later Bgde. The relief was to be carried out by Horse-Batteries, and the first half was completed during the afternoon and evening. The personnel of the Horse-Batteries relieved proceeded to their respective Wagon Lines.	
9/10/16	Remainder of relief completed by 2 P.M., when the remaining Horse Brigade Staffs, and Batteries were Carried by Lorries and train to join their Wagon Lines. 2 Lt. H.B. Thompson RFA Bgde Staff was sent	

Army Form C. 2118.

WAR DIARY
or
INTELLIGENCE SUMMARY   SHEET 11

(Erase heading not required.)

Instructions regarding War Diaries and Intelligence Summaries are contained in F.S. Regs., Part II. and the Staff Manual respectively. Title pages will be prepared in manuscript.

Hour, Date, Place	Summary of Events and Information	Remarks and references to Appendices
YPRES 9/10/16	to SALEUX to make arrangements in advance, and to superintend detrainment on arrival at the Station. Brigade H.Q's been handed over to Lt. Col M R J Conway R.F.A. to Lt. Col Cochrane D.S.O. R.F.A. 277th Bgde 55th D.A. During the night both the 10th and 97th Bty's marched out en route to PROVEN for the purpose of entrainment in the Early hours of the morning. The Brigade Headquarter Staff and D/147th Battery remained in then began train during the night.	Weather fine
MARCH TO 10/10/16. 2 AM 5 AM	10th Bty departed by train. 97th Bty departed by train.	
THE SOMME DISTRICT	Both Batteries detrained at SALEUX and immediately marched to "A" Camp (half-way between BUIRE and LAVIEVILLE) variously arriving there on its way by the 11th. Its route being outskirts of AMIENS, CAMON, DAOURS, LA NEUVILLE, HEILLY RIBEMONT, BUIRE to "A" Camp.	Weather fine
11.30. AM	Brigade Headquarters and D/147th Bty entrained and left SALEUX where then detrained in the early hours of the 11th.	
11/10/16. 8.30 AM	Brigade Headquarters and D/147th Bty R.H.Q. marched to DAOURS via outskirts of AMIENS, CAMON to DAOURS Y/L. Weather was threatening and some rain fell during the	

Army Form C. 2118.

WAR DIARY
or
INTELLIGENCE SUMMARY   SHEET III

(Erase heading not required.)

Hour, Date, Place	Summary of Events and Information	Remarks and references to Appendices
MARCH TO SOMME DISTRICT. 11/10/16	Morning but cleared in the afternoon. The night was spent in the village. 10th and 97th Batteries having previously arrived at "A" Camp remained there till the concentration of 29th Divisional Artillery was completed.	
12/10/16 8.30 AM	The Headquarters Staffs and D/147th Bty in Concours with Staffs of 17th and 15th Bgdes, D/17 Bde, 460th Bty marched to "A" Camp. Here by the time its whole of the 29th Div Arty had concentrated prior to moving off next day to their positions on the SOMME FRONT. D.A.H.Q. were also situated here. Lt. Brig Gen Malcolm Peake was absent in England on sick leave. The troops were temporarily accommodated in large huts and the officers in tents. The weather still remained fine but had become much colder. The night was spent here by the Brigade.	
13/10/16 6 AM	Lt. Col. M.R.J. Comegs RFA, the Orderly Officer, Signallers and Liaison of the Brigade Staff, Battery Commanders, each with an Officer & men of their Batteries, with their respective Battery Staffs marched to take over positions from the 62nd Bgde RFA 41st Div Arty, which were to be relieved by half-Batteries on that and the following days. The above Officers made the usual taking over	

Army Form C. 2118.

WAR DIARY
or
INTELLIGENCE SUMMARY SHEET IV

(Erase heading not required.)

Instructions regarding War Diaries and Intelligence Summaries are contained in F.S. Regs., Part II. and the Staff Manual respectively. Title pages will be prepared in manuscript.

Hour, Date, Place	Summary of Events and Information	Remarks and references to Appendices
13/10/16. 2.P.M SOMME FRONT	Movements. Lt C.J. Costello 10th Bty. returned to "A" Camp in instruction for the Brigade Headquarters, together with the Hdq. Battalion B/70th and 97th. to move forward. The latter marched out from "A" Camp to their respective position, which were as follows Trench Map France Sheet 57°C S.N. 20 svo — Relays. H.Q. 147th Bde. relieved H.Q. 62nd Bde RFA at S.23.a.07 10th Bty RFA — A/62 Bty RFA — T.7.a. 27 97th Bty — B/62 — T.7.a. 25.80 D/147 — D/62 — T.7.a. 55 Route taken "A" Camp. ALBERT. FRICOURT. MAMETZ. MONTAUBAN. The weather was fine with a brilliant Moonlight night. Men & the roads were in a very bad condition, and as MONTAUBAN was approached the road became more difficult for traffic.	
14/10/16.	Remainder of relief completed during the night — the 147th Brigade coming under the administration 5th H.Q. Staff. 30th Bn. Bn. and covering its front by S.O.S punkins N 20.d. 9.a. to N 20.d. 77. Day spent in established Brigade in her position and the usual amount of ammunition expended in day and night operations 10th Bty. had 2 drivers wounded. ×	× No 62305 Dr RAYBURN G No 629 & Dr RAVELLY A. (Both reported shortly afterwards)

WAR DIARY
or
INTELLIGENCE SUMMARY

SHEET V

Army Form C. 2118.

(Erase heading not required.)

Hour, Date, Place	Summary of Events and Information	Remarks and references to Appendices
SOMME FRONT. 15/10/16	Further time spent in Gun and Wagon lines - The latter being outside but position. Weather was a little cooler & am kind in the former, heavier still finer breeze. Thunderous and frosty during the night. LIME TRENCH bombarded by Batteries of the Brigade from 4 P.M. & 5 P.M. rate of fire being 1 rd. the gun per second min. + 1 gun + relief. 1 section B.Ldr slightly wounded (10th Bty.) After a [?] Operation on our right the line was strengthened in the vicinity of MILD TRENCH.	+ No.77351 D. HARMAN. (killed) No. 21475 a/Bdr Stitch slightly wounded.
16/10/16.	Weather fine and cold with mist clearing the night and morning. LIME TRENCH again bombarded from 4 P.M. to 5 P.M. from the two new sites the 18th Battn. had considerable trouble with their guns due mainly to weak springs and excessive use. R+Q. + gunners were handed over to them by A/277 Bty., and these men were Capts. F. Lieutenant a rapid state of fire. On the day, P.R. Itees are sent to Ordnance with their main sides. Gone. When leaving 3 guns in action 1. 4.5 How. B D/147 was also sent to Ordnance. The roads and tracks generally are so inundated with shell holes, that all ammunition & necessity to be carried in packs. The brivis return to lines with hack to ammunition.	

Army Form C. 2118.

WAR DIARY
or
INTELLIGENCE SUMMARY.
(Erase heading not required.)

Sheet VI

Place	Date	Hour	Summary of Events and Information	Remarks and references to Appendices
SOMME FRONT	16/10/16		2 Lt. E.E. Barrs rejoined D/147th Bty from 30th D.A. 1 Driver and 1 Gunner wounded 97th Bty.	16/10/16 97th Bty. No 32479 Gr SUELSON (bullet) No 12247 Gr EVANS H (wounded) No 74666 Gr ORR D. wounded No 33651 Gr DYSON A (foot)
	17/10/16		Usual Bombardments carried out during the day. Fine during the day, but rain fell throughout the night and made operations for the following day difficult. 1 O.R. 97th Bty wounded. Ammunition expended noon 16/10/16 to noon 17/10/16. 152. Shrapnel 555 H.E. 398 4.5 H.E.	17/10/16 97th Bty No 43992 Gr WAITE C.H.
	18/10/16		At an early hour before light the Division on our right attacked and advanced on front 500 yds on a front of 700 yds. – GREASE TRENCH taken. 2 Officers and 102 Other ranks captured. The Brigade supplied a Creeping Barrage on own front in support of the above operation. Ammunition expended from 17/10/16 to noon 18/10/16 96 Shrapnel 289 H.E. – 2 of our guns B 10th Bty out of action – 1 with broken spring, the other with "A" Tube. These leaves three 1 Gun in action	
	19/10/16		A normal day – battles from here onwards unsettled – rain frequent and countryside rendered very difficult for traffic. Ammunition expended noon 18/10/16 to noon 19/10/16 60 Shrapnel 53 H.E. 126 4.5 H.E.	
	20/10/16		Battries heavily shelled throughout the day and Brigade line is continually cut – the remaining gun B 10th Bty knocked out then putting the Battery completely out of action	

Army Form C. 2118.

WAR DIARY
or
INTELLIGENCE SUMMARY.
(Erase heading not required.)

SHEET VII

Instructions regarding War Diaries and Intelligence Summaries are contained in F.S. Regs., Part II and the Staff Manual respectively. Title pages will be prepared in manuscript.

Place	Date	Hour	Summary of Events and Information	Remarks and references to Appendices
SOMME FRONT	20/10/16		Casualties 3 other Ranks (10th Bty) wounded - 1 O.R. slightly wounded (97 H. Bty).	10th Bty. 1 O.R. 20/10/16 No 35166 Gnr HOPKINSON C No 10348 Gnr KENEH F No 85143 Gnr WILKINS H. No 50659 Bdr BOTTLE C (97th) No 16001 Bdr HOLDSWORTH W D/147.
	21/10/16		1 O.R. slightly wounded (D/147th Bty). Ammunition expended noon 20/10/16 to noon 21/10/16 60 Shrapnel. H.E. 30 4.5 H.E. Battery again heavily shelled - Casualties 2 Lt F.G. Lockwood D/147 Bty wounded 5 other ranks wounded. 1 O.R. missing - Lt R.C. Donnelly 97th Bty killed and 5 O.R.'s wounded - 2 Lt K.R. Park 10th Bty wounded and 2 O.R.'s wounded Ammunition expended noon 21/10/16 to noon 22/10/16 60 H.E. 309 4.5 H.E.	
	22/10/16		Day fine. No' mists during the morning - D/147 Bty 4 hours in action. A normal day - Ammunition expended 81 Shrapnel 419 H.E. 538 H.E. (4.5) Battn unmolested. Capt MacGill Q.V.C. evacuated sick to hospital.	
	23/10/16		Thick fog which did not clear till noon - MILD TRENCH taken by Division on right during the evening. 97th Bty in action in the afternoon. 97th Bty. relieve D/147 Bty wounded, up by enemy in front of GUEUDECOURT. 2Lt J.C. Hutton D/147 Bty wounded, when returning from O.P. Ammunition expended 22/10/16 to noon 23/10/16. 469 H.E. 55 4.5 H.E.	
	24/10/16		Very wet during night and throughout the day - Roads rendered very difficult for transport & even trick. Ammunition expended noon 23/10/16 to noon 24/10/16. 241 AM H.E. 167 H.E. (4.5)	

Army Form C. 2118.

WAR DIARY
or
INTELLIGENCE SUMMARY

SHEET VIII

(Erase heading not required.)

Instructions regarding War Diaries and Intelligence Summaries are contained in F.S. Regs., Part II. and the Staff Manual respectively. Title pages will be prepared in manuscript.

Hour, Date, Place	Summary of Events and Information	Remarks and references to Appendices
SOMME FRONT 25/10/16	Wet. Important operation, which should have taken place on this day, postponed till 28th. Fairly quiet. Ammunition expended in preceding 24 hours 204 rds HE. 193 4·5 HE.	Casualties to other Ranks 21/10/16 WOUNDED No 4834 Gnr KEAM W D/147 No 77580 Gnr DAVIES A 10th Bde No 32860 Gnr COUPLAND J 10th Bde No 48332 Sgt McKENZIE H 97th Bde No 62544 Bmb ROBERTS N — No 56576 Gnr LANE R J — No 25235 — MILLS W — No 60142 Sgt JOHN E G — No 16210 Sgt RABY F D/147 Bty No 2118 Cpl SARGENT S — No 110068 Gnr CANNINGS S — No 88725 Bdr BUCK A — No 56147 Gr. COLL J — (missing)
26/10/16	Further wet weather. By this time the countryside and roads had become so saturated that operation of any importance were out of the question. When possible bombardments of particular points & trenches, sap heads and roads with a view to spoil operations in the future, but this was the only shooting possible. Ammunition expended during last 24 hours 60 Shrapnel. 180 HE. 248 4·5" HE	
27/10/16	Heavy showers throughout the day & night, as far as the tactical situation was concerned was normal. 2 Lt J C Johnstone posted from 29th DAC to 10th Bde RFA 2 Lt Y Williams — " — — D/147 Bde RFA 2 Lt C D Cooper — " — — D/147 Bde RFA Ammunition expended 186 HE 256 4·5 HE	
28/10/16	More rain. Operation again postponed to Nov 1. 1 Gun B 97th Bde out of action with break springs. Situation still normal. Capt B H O Holmes RFA slightly wounded but remained at duty. Ammunition expended 61 Shrapnel 332 HE. 222 4·5" HE	

WAR DIARY or INTELLIGENCE SUMMARY

Army Form C. 2118.

SHEET IX

Hour, Date, Place	Summary of Events and Information	Remarks and references to Appendices
SOMME FRONT 29/10/16	10th Bty. which had been out of action since their remaining gun was knocked out, moved up 5 guns ready for action to a new position about 500 yds to the left, near B/Bty's old position. The gun still remaining at advance under repair. Another 2 guns had been supplied to the 2 Bty. guns deficient. Whilst the remainder had been through, overhauled and new tarp hoisted. Wire necessary Telephonic Communication was also established but later B Cover from the Batteries, however, the whole Battery moves into the position until proper Covering could be obtained. Ammunition defended 67 Shrapnel 180 HE 160 4.5 HE.	Casualties to other Ranks 21/10/16. WOUNDED. Gr. KEAM. W. D/147. No.48839 No.77560 Bm. DAVIES A. 10th Bty. No.32860 Gr. COUPLAND J. 10th Bty. No.48332 Sqt. Mc. KENZIE H. 97th Bty. No.62544 Rdr. ROBERTS. N. — No.56576 Gnr. LANE R.J. — No.25235 " MILLS W — No.80143 Sgt. Jones F.G. — No.16210 Sgt. RABY F. b/147 Bty. No.2118 CPL. SARGENT. G — No.110068 Gnr. CANNINGS. S — No.28775 Bdr. BUCK. A. — No.56147 Gr. COLE. J. — (missing)
30/10/16	Own heavy rain thro'out the afternoon. 18 Divn. & 5 Gunners Jones from the Base. Tactical situation unchanged - Night of 30/31 29th Division relieved in the line by 1st Australian Division. Ammunition Defended 231 H.E. 128 4.5 H.E.	
31/10/16	Normal day. Line the duel in the morning wet during the afternoon - Lt J.L. Sullivan A.V.C. noted to the Brigade vice Capt. Mac Gill evacuated sick. Ammunition Defended 180 H.E. 48 4.5 H.E.	

W.R. George
Lieut Col
Comdg 2nd 147 Bg DC

29th Division.

147th BRIGADE

R. F. A.

NOVEMBER 1 9 1 6

CONFIDENTIAL

War Diary

147th Brigade RFA

From   Nov 1st

To   Nov 30th

(Volume V)

Army Form C. 2118.

WAR DIARY
or
INTELLIGENCE SUMMARY
(Erase heading not required.)

Sheet 1

Instructions regarding War Diaries and Intelligence Summaries are contained in F.S. Regs., Part II. and the Staff Manual respectively. Title Pages will be prepared in manuscript.

Place	Date	Hour	Summary of Events and Information	Remarks and references to Appendices
VICINITY OF LONGUEVAL	1/11/16		Weather unsettled. In view of the attempt to clean up situation in N.20.d, D/147th Bty assisted in an hours bombardment in LARD TRENCH. 97th Bty also fired about 60 rds for the purpose of catching any runners who might attempt to escape from the trench. The bombardment was repeated again at 11.A.M. During the course of the morning, Battery Positions were inspected by Brig. Gen. Malcolm Peake C.M.G. B.G.R.A. 29th D.A. No. 19483 Corporal J Kitchen 10th Bty R.F.A slightly wounded in front shin. No. 48034 Gnr W Hannaford 97th Bty also wounded (shell shock). Ammunition expended noon 31/10/16 to noon 1/11/16. 234.A. 250 AX. 402 BX.	
	2/11/16		Weather still unsettled and rain at intervals. Bombardment of Nov 1st in LARD TRENCH repeated at 7.A.M. and 10.A.M. Bdy Stn was horsed. No. 121850 Gunner G Page 10th Bty wounded (G.S.W.) Rounds expended noon 1/11/16 to noon 2/11/16 150.A 330.AX 435 BX	
	3/11/16		An occasional shower but the weather showed signs of improvement. LARD TRENCH again bombarded at 12 noon. All operations for the proposed Minor Operations by the 5th Divn. 5th Bde ground and knocked the Operation to clean up situation in N.20.d. Were arranged for. Early news from G.H. 5th Inst., whilst the Major Operation that was to have taken place on the 25th Oct has now been postponed indefinitely. Ammunition expended noon 2/11/16 to noon 3/11/16 207.A 150 AX. 296 BX	

WAR DIARY
or
INTELLIGENCE SUMMARY

Army Form C. 2118.

Sheet II

Place	Date	Hour	Summary of Events and Information	Remarks and references to Appendices
VICINITY OF LONGUEVAL	4/11/16		Fine during the day but rain fell at night and much hampered the operation in the following day. 4 P.M. LARD TRENCH again bombarded. Ammunition expended 161 A. 192 AX. 257 BX.	
	5/11/16		The Brigade assisted 1st Australian Division in their attempt to join up their line with N.W. end B. BISCUIT TRENCH to Jct at N. end B GREASE TRENCH, their line with a view to taking Jct with line eastwards LARD TRENCH and defence system between these points.	
		12.30	Attack began in heavy rain. Some batteries of LARD TRENCH was taken but could not be held & further attempt was made at 2.15 P.M. but the troops equally unsuccessful. The operation was much handicapped by weather conditions and rain & the trenches being below the crest, the barrage could not give sufficient support. In the present and in operations in our left the hidden condition of the ground made it almost impossible for the infantry to keep up with the Barrage. Rest of the day however. 2 Sergts, 1 Cpl., 3 Bdrs., 2 a/Bdrs., 7 Gunners and 2 Drivers joined from the Base. No 51043 Cpl Bedford N. wounded (9 S.W.) Ammunition expended from 4/11/16 to hour 5/11/16. 776 A 508 AX. 680 BX. From 2nd to 5th Hostile aeroplanes very active over DELVILLE VALLEY	
	6/11/16		Weather unsettled - a normal day. 2 shells pitched nr 15th Battery line. No 40635 Gnr A Gibson 10th Bty (9 S.W.) wounded. 2 Other Ranks No 108662 Gnr 1 Sgt ! Cummings R and No 40635 Gnr A Gibson 10 Bty (9 S.W.) 1 Sgt ! Driver hotel from the Base. Ammunition expended hour 5/11/16 to hour 6/11/16 150 A 180 AX 48 BX	

Army Form C. 2118.

WAR DIARY
or
INTELLIGENCE SUMMARY

(Erase heading not required.)

Sheet III

Instructions regarding War Diaries and Intelligence Summaries are contained in F.S. Regs., Part II. and the Staff Manual respectively. Title Pages will be prepared in manuscript.

Place	Date	Hour	Summary of Events and Information	Remarks and references to Appendices
VICINITY OF LONGUEVAL	7/11/16	14.00	Occasional showers and roads still in a very heavy condition. "Chinese Bombardment" carried out in Brigade zone. Otherwise nothing of importance occurred. Ammunition expended noon 6/11/16 to noon 7/11/16 281 A 336 AX, 12S BX	
	8/11/16		Normal, with weather still inclined to be wet. 1 Howr. gun sent from base and posted to D/147th Bty RYA except for an occasional Barrage on our front line. Hostile Arty fairly quiet. Ammunition expended 140 A 180 AX 48 BX (from noon 7/11/16 to noon 8/11/16	
	9/11/16		Still wet fine - Enemy Artillery batteries more active in DELVILLE VALLEY, but no damage done. Own Hostile Aerial activity may marked during the morning. Ammunition expended noon 8/11/16 to noon 9/11/16 150 A 180 AX, 71 BX.	
	10/11/16		Weather still in an unsettled state. Tactical situation unchanged. Hostile aeroplanes very active over DELVILLE VALLEY and roads in S.12.A and T.7.d. upon which they fired with Machine Guns. 2Lt. H Monro bought RYA posted from Y.29 T.M. Battery to 76th Bty RYA. Rds. expended 258 A. 5AX 48 AX	
	11/11/16		Weather dull - a normal day. 2Lt C.E.P. Gram RYA posted from Base to 99th Bty RYA. Capt A.S. Hindu's RAMC M.O. i/c 147th Bgde RYA sent on leave and his place taken temporally [temporarily] filled by Capt. J.R. Pollin RAMC from 89th Field Ambulance. Rds. expended from noon 10/11/16 to noon 11/11/16 230 A 48 BX	

WAR DIARY or INTELLIGENCE SUMMARY

Army Form C. 2118.

Sheet IV

Place	Date	Hour	Summary of Events and Information	Remarks and references to Appendices
VICINITY OF LONGUEVAL	12/11/16		Fine but cloudy in parts. Roads in shattered places ankle deep in mud. Nothing of tactical importance occurred and generally quiet in vicinity. Battery Position. Lt J L Sullivan AVC evacuated sick to hospital. Hostile aeroplane active. Rds expended noon 11/11/16 to 12/11/16 653 A. 165 A x 337 BX	
	13/11/16		Fine, thick and becoming colder. Chinese Bombardment carried out on our front. 12 rds 10.5 cm fired on D/147 Bty Position and resulted in No. 31699 Gnr G Coleman B/Nor Battn being killed. Gnr O'Kane greatest Ammunition expended 841 A. 69 A x 192 BX	
	14/11/16		Fine and much colder. Hostile Artillery here active. Creeping Barrage suffering in conjunction with Operation on our left. The latter was partially successful — the left Sector gaining their objective, the middle sector partial objective, shell the right sector was held up. 97th Bty was shelled and its gun howitzers blown broke were wounded No. 50659 Pte C. B/111/2. No. 51525 Gnr M McGowan, No. 58348 Gnr L. Edwards, No. 38304 a/Bdr H Williams all B 97th Bty. No. 116367 Gnr Atkin HQ D/147 Bty also slightly wounded but remained at duty. Rds expended noon 13/11/16 to noon 14/11/16 150 A. 180 A x 48 BX	
LES BOEUFFS	15/11/16		Very cold - frost during night and temperature very low about freezing point during the day. Hostile artillery active on our front line. Enemy planes very active & flying low. 1 plane brought down in flames last k noon 15/11/16 330 A. 48 B x Ammunition expended noon 14/11/16	

2449 Wt. W14957/M90 750,000 1/16 J.B.C. & A. Forms/C.2118/12.

Army Form C. 2118.

WAR DIARY
or
INTELLIGENCE SUMMARY
(Erase heading not required.)

Sheet V

Place	Date	Hour	Summary of Events and Information	Remarks and references to Appendices
VICINITY OF LONGUEVAL	16/11/16		Cold and frosty. 8 gunners and 1 driver joined from the Base. No 111259 Gr. J. Anderson D/147th Bty. accidentally killed. Enemy aeroplane brought down and landed near SWITCH TRENCH. Quiet day. Rounds expended 262.A. 90 AX. 48 BX.	
	17/11/16		Still cold and frosty. Ground now frozen and render difficult to horses. Excellent shooting in a group at N.3.c.6.2. by D/147th Bty. RFA. Shot registered a direct hit and destroyed 4 parts of German making their scale in an increased alert — Quiet in the vicinity of the Battery Positions. Ammunition expended noon 16/11/16 to noon 17/11/16 234 A. 1 AX. 88 BX	
	18/11/16		Snow during the night but in the morning this turned to rain. Wheat continued most of the day. Nothing of tactical importance occurred. 35th Div Artillery relieved by 1st Australian Div Artillery — The Brigade then comes under the administration of the latter. Rds expended 17/11/16 to 18/11/16 300 A. 30 AX. 48 BX	
	19/11/16		Wet, the dull — Quiet on our sector of the front — Ammunition expended 330 AX 155 BX from noon 18/11/16 to noon 19/11/16.	
	20/11/16		Dull weather but no rain — a normal day. Information received that 2 Lt. Dix Arty. been to be withdrawn from the line by night B 24/25th. No 6901 Gnr. R Jenkins 16th Bty. RFA accidentally killed. Capt. J.M. Cross A.V.C. posted from Base to 147th Bgde RFA vice Lt. J.L. Sullivan A.V.C. evacuated to hospital. 2 Corporals promoted to Sgts. - 3 Bdrs promoted Corporal - 5 a/Bdrs from Shrt B.shoe Rds expended noon 19/11/16 to noon 20/11/16 148 A. 304 AX. 76 BX	

Army Form C. 2118.

WAR DIARY
or
INTELLIGENCE SUMMARY
(Erase heading not required.)

Sheet VI

Instructions regarding War Diaries and Intelligence Summaries are contained in F. S. Regs., Part II. and the Staff Manual respectively. Title Pages will be prepared in manuscript.

Place	Date	Hour	Summary of Events and Information	Remarks and references to Appendices
VICINITY OF LONGUEVAL	21/11/16		Against front, mist in the morning, but clear in the afternoon. Much aerial activity on both sides. Own planes brought down. Except for a short and keen Barrage put up in front of GUEUDECOURT Guns quiet on our front. 2 Lt N A Stephenson posted to 97th Bty RFA. 2 Lt. A.B. Knight posted to D/147 Bde RFA. Left from Base Ammunition expended 150 A 240 AX 148 BX hours 20/11/16 to hour 21/11/16.	
	22/11/16		Own guns with a mist in the morning - brilliant sunshine in the afternoon. Much combats in the air - 1 German and 1 British Plane brought down. 2 Lt C.E.P. Gray evacuated to hospital. 2 Lt F. Williams D/147 Bde RFA posted to 29th D.A.C. 10th Bde RFA relieved in the line by 24th Australian Bty. Expenditure Ammunition to their Wagon lines Ammunition expended hour 21/11/16 to hour 22/11/16. 292 A 206 AX 258 BX	
	23/11/16		Slight but down bright - a very fine day. Continued activity in the air. Enemy quiet. 1 section of 97th Bde RFA withdrawn to their Wagon lines. Major H Dinnes 10th Bde RFA proceeded on leave to England. Ammunition expended hour 22/11/16 to hour 23/11/16. 180 AX 302 BX	
	24/11/16		A fine day - 1 section of 97th Bde and 1 section of D/147th Bde withdrawn from the line. Ammunition expended hour 23/11/16 to hour 24/11/16. 50AX 51 BX	

WAR DIARY or INTELLIGENCE SUMMARY

Army Form C. 2118.

Sheet VII

Place	Date	Hour	Summary of Events and Information	Remarks and references to Appendices
LOCALITY OF LONGUEVAL	25/11/16		Remaining Section of D/147 Bty and 97th Bty withdrawn to Wagon Lines. D/147 Battery handed over their ammunition to 101st Australian Bty, whilst 97th Bty handed over ammunition to Batteries 21st Australian Field Artillery Brigade. Lt. Col. M.R.J. Cruikshank, Commanding the Brigade, was evacuated sick to hospital with throat trouble. 97 caused for the most part by the day.	
E 28 near MÉAULTE	26/11/16		Rain early in the morning, but fine later. Brigade marched out from Wagon Lines to E 28 Cavalry Camp near MÉAULTE, route MONTAUBAN, CARNOY, outskirts of FRICOURT, MÉAULTE. CAVALRY CAMP E 28. The whole of 29th Divl Arty was concentrated there. Owing to the heavy condition of the ground & the hour at which Wagon lines were much delayed & was caused in the early portion of the march, which proved satisfactory, after 'COSY CORNER' MONTAUBAN was passed. Unit marched independently and its destination was reached during the course of the afternoon.	
	27/11/16		Fine with frost at night. Day spent quietly, and attempts made to improve shelters and stop leaks, since the accommodation on arrival was found quite inadequate.	
	28/11/16		Fine and cold. Still frost. With a view to taking on new Wagon lines at A.I.R a party of 1 Officer, 1 NCO and 6 other Ranks (the latter from each Unit) proceeded and made the usual taking over preparations from the 336 Brigade R.F.A 8th Divl. Arty.	

Army Form C. 2118.

WAR DIARY
or
INTELLIGENCE SUMMARY

(Erase heading not required.)

Sheet VIII

Place	Date	Hour	Summary of Events and Information	Remarks and references to Appendices
A.I.D.	29/11/16	11-15	Cold and frosty. Brigade with Batteries at 300 yds interval marched viâ MEAVLTEL, MAMETZ, to A.I.D. It has begun take position and arrived there during the course of the afternoon.	
	30/11/16		Cold and frosty. Day spent in unknown new horse lines. Shed and is in very muddy and dirty condition. Men have musarus & leaven his dere have granted to the Brigade.	

Q.F. Knight Lt. RFA
Adjnt 147th Bde RFA

29th Division.

147th BRIGADE

R. F. A.

DECEMBER 1 9 1 6

Vol 10

CONFIDENTIAL

WAR DIARY

147th BRIGADE. RFA

DEC 1st TO DEC 31st

(VOL. 10)

Army Form C. 2118.

WAR DIARY
or
INTELLIGENCE SUMMARY

Sheet I

(Erase heading not required.)

Instructions regarding War Diaries and Intelligence Summaries are contained in F.S. Regs., Part II. and the Staff Manual respectively. Title Pages will be prepared in manuscript.

Place	Date	Hour	Summary of Events and Information	Remarks and references to Appendices
A.i.d in Vicinity of MONTAUBAN	1/13/16		Quiet. Battery Commanders visit the French Battery positions which the 15th and 147th Brigades are taking on on the night 6th/7th. Time spent in attempts to behave hors Wagon lines which were in an attacking condition.	
	2/4/16		Still quiet. Work in Wagon lines continues. From this date the 6th hot ammunition was daily carried to New Battery Positions and dumped there, with a team in charge until the arrival of the Brigades on night 6th/7th. Major H. Dixon DSO RFA rejoins 10th Bty RFA from leave in England.	
	3/4/16		Brigade Commander Lt M R.Y. Connap RFA rejoins from Rest Billets. Capt. G.S. Hastie RAMC M.O/c 147th Bde RFA rejoins from leave in England. Capt Allin RAMC returned to 89th Field Ambulance. Still fine. Work in Wagon lines - weather still fresh.	
	4/4/16		Quiet. No damage in the forenoon. Afternoon taking up ammunition to new position. No 85054 Bdr N HODGSON 10th Bty wounded by bomb splinters. Lt C.Y. Castell 10th Bty RFA evacuated sick to hospital - recent mic on knee-turn.	
	5/4/16		Quiet sets in and weather rouses and remains dispersed for transport.	

Army Form C. 2118.

WAR DIARY
or
INTELLIGENCE SUMMARY

Sheet II

(Erase heading not required.)

Instructions regarding War Diaries and Intelligence Summaries are contained in F.S. Regs., Part II. and the Staff Manual respectively. Title Pages will be prepared in manuscript.

Place	Date	Hour	Summary of Events and Information	Remarks and references to Appendices
MAP Ref FRANCE 57c S.W. H.Q at TROOP H.Q Battalion vicinity of T.16.	6/9/16		Morning spent in preparation to move. Battalion of 1st Bgde R.H.A. and 147th Bde R.H.A. have not set the bus and taken over from the French. The Heads. Quarters of the Brigades, with their Inspection Batteries, were carried forward to join 6th Light Front Sheet and are responsible for the line from 6 p.m. on the 6th. Lt Col N.H.C. SHERBROOKE takes Command of Light Front R.A. under the tactical and administrative Artillery Headquarters shall not be seen. 17th Bgde R.A. observed on east	
	7/9/16		Registrations in ran were made but front mush hampered by bad light. Salient 6 Front covered in Left Front R.A. U89. 9 9½ — O.31 c.5.3. Shot on Covered in 5.18pm. Batteries and L 4.5 How. Batteries — day fairly quiet.	
	8/9/16		Your own cable with some mist - registration was to had light again different from in no Sect. above normal but no casualties. Major Bell proceeded on leave to England. Both batteries fire how onwards 127 who the Batter ration of 3A x 1A.	
	9/9/16		Bad light but some registration done. Grant established with casualties for in enemy in reply to their shelling our front line. MORVAL and COMBLES shelled during the day.	
	10/9/16		Very cold, slight snow but more turning to rain later. Light jarr good & limited further registration. Unknown hostile Bgth batteries were also displaced.	

WAR DIARY or INTELLIGENCE SUMMARY

Army Form C. 2118.

Place	Date	Hour	Summary of Events and Information	Remarks and references to Appendices
Map FRANCE 57C SW HQ T.20 d.4.0 Battery in vicinity B.T.16.	10/12/16		1 Shell fell in Ammunition Dump of 97th Bty RYA and destroyed 185 rds A. and 26 rds who ax. at the same time putting one gun out of action. No casualties to personnel. Capt A. M. McAeski M.B. RYA reported 97th Bty RYA from leave. 2 Lt C.E.P. Shaw RYA reported 97 Bty RYA from Field Ambulance. Capt A.O. Hopkins RYA D/147 Bty RYA proceeded on a Course of Gunnery Instruction to England	
	11/12/16		Situation normal.	
	12/12/16		9/10 cm slow bombardment carried on in the afternoon. Very war-observation bad. Kermit day and held firm. Brig General Malcolm Peake C.M.G. having been authorized to command 51 Corps Artillery visited Group Headquarters and Battery Position of the Impre Group. Reports that HE. bombardment just 1 gun B 97th Bty RYA at of action. Brigade Command Lt Col M.R.J. Donnage goes on leave to England.	
	13/12/16		Fine morning, wet afternoon. A normal day. 2/Lt C.B. Cooper D/147 Bty RYA rejoins his Battery from leave to England	
	14/12/16		Rained heavily all day - but light made observation impossible during the morning a bombardment was carried out on the function in South Kommen with good effect. Our Shrapnel normal.	
	15/12/16		Situation normal. Going to rain later and inclined to be misty. Usual firing on tracks in back ares. No. 95554 G/Br. JUDD D/147th Bty wounded in Right thigh by Shrapnel from gun information regarding his Brethren relief having been obtained. Catkin road and back was shelled from 4.30 PM to 11 PM day 6th knob tunnel 2 AM.	
	17/12/16		Morrowth 97th Bty RYA rejoin 97th Bty RYA from leave to England	

WAR DIARY or INTELLIGENCE SUMMARY

Army Form C. 2118.

Sheet IV

Place	Date	Hour	Summary of Events and Information	Remarks and references to Appendices
Map FRANCE 57 C.S.W. H.Q. T.20 d.40	18/10/16		Misty and hot in the morning — fine later — a normal day.	
	19/10/16		Fine. Observation permitted some arty. activity later down — usual day and night firing.	
Battery Positions in Vicinity of T.16	20/10/16		Fine. Continues — no firing normal — a few enemy shells fell in vicinity of Battery positions. No. 62709. Gnr Q. LATHBURY 97th Bty R.F.A. dangerously wounded by a piece of H.E. – He died of wounds on the following day in brother hands and became Funerated.	
	21/10/16		Bg. Gnr. MALCOLM inspected with some care en at which Bg. Gnr. Acting Commanding 29th D.A. vis. Bg. Gnr. Malcolm Peake CMG with Qrt. Head quarters and Battery Positions. 16 L.D.H. and 3 R.H. horses received from Remount Depot. Situation normal.	
	22/10/16		Some rain during the morning. Shewing fire Registration and bombardment firing made during clear hour of afternoon owing to objective being clearly and brightly from in back areas and back behind enemy trenches.	
	23/10/16		Weather unsettled. Very strong wind and some rain. 1:30 P.M. to 3:30 P.M. bombardment in enemy trenches 4:30 to 5:30 P.M. Burst 8 guns in each Battery from LE MESNIL to enemy front line from 22/12/16 ex. for relation of ammunition in Crassal. 62 A 157 AX for Battr. Battr. 8r.12 Bx for 4 S. How. Battr.	

WAR DIARY or INTELLIGENCE SUMMARY

Army Form C. 2118.

Sheet V

(Erase heading not required.)

Instructions regarding War Diaries and Intelligence Summaries are contained in F.S. Regs., Part II. and the Staff Manual respectively. Title Pages will be prepared in manuscript.

Place	Date	Hour	Summary of Events and Information	Remarks and references to Appendices
MAP FRANCE 57.0.S.W H.Q. T20.d.4.0. Battn in trenches B.T.6.	24/9/16		Wet and misty. Gun at intervals - heavy winds. 13.30 to 15.30 bombardment carried out on Enemy trenches - bursts good on some objectives from 16.30 to 17.30. 20.00 Enemy put up a Heavy Barrage in the front line and sub/sec trenches. Lys Gent & Replied but Heavy Retaliation and Enemy ceased fire soon after.	
	25/9/16		Dull and windy. Two Short bombardments fired in Left front. One at 08.30 to 06.45 the other 11.30 to 11.45. Generally effective good direction and bursts were obtained. On each occasion the Enemy replied with a heavy burst of fire on our front line and Sutton & Grenades. 20.00 to 21.00 tracks leading to & heavy front line shelled intermittently in supposition that a German relief was taking place Gas Shells were used. Two Officers were posted to the Brigade from the Base and were attached as follows. 2Lt J R Knight to D/147" 10th Bde. R.Y.A. 2Lt Q R Kilbn to " D/147" Bde. R.Y.A.	
	26/9/16		Fine during morning. Some rain in the afternoon. 12-15.59 Continuous bombardment of Enemy trench system. Heavy hostile retaliation was given from 13.00 to 15.00 but ceased after that time. The Shell burst well and the fire effect good. Gas Shells used.	

WAR DIARY or INTELLIGENCE SUMMARY

Army Form C. 2118.

Sheet VI

Instructions regarding War Diaries and Intelligence Summaries are contained in F.S. Regs, Part II. and the Staff Manual respectively. Title Pages will be prepared in manuscript.

(Erase heading not required.)

Place	Date	Hour	Summary of Events and Information	Remarks and references to Appendices
Map FRANCE 57c S.W. HQ T.20 d.40 Battery Position in Vichete B T.16.	27/10/16		A fine day on the whole. Inclined to be hot. In the afternoon a normal day.	
	28/10/16		152 locally dull and uncertain. First in the morning turning to rain late. 1st Bgde RHA relieved in the line by 17th Bgde R.F.A. Lt Col H.E.W. Mansell R.H.A. 330 RGA Command and L.t Col N.H.C. Sherbrooke RHA Smith Palmer Command B/L295 Grant R.A. vice L.t Col N.H.C. Sherbrooke RHA. 26 Gunners join from the Base. A normal day.	
	29/10/16		Weather still unsettled. Some rain - wind - cloud. Saps for frontage two Brigades always tends to fine. Fires were lit in Enemy lines & Communication during the night.	
	30/10/16		Kept in the morning - fine - the unsettled for the remainder of the day. Intense bombardment carried out in enemy trenches. French Effective. And fire was well directed. Day otherwise normal but as usual. Bombardment at 11 a.m. - faint, effective. In hostile trenches, line E opened them up in Baasha -	
	31/10/16		Since April with the exception of a few days when changing positions two brigades have been continuously in the line and since June has had night firing all the time -- In the last 3 months the condition of the wagon lines has been very bad. So has there being leaving in mud and wet to 20 hrs of the later time been landed with during the last 3 weeks. The Health of the men has been kept considering the constant strain & little sickness in the Gun line --	

Sd R (indecipherable)
Lt Col Commdg
COMDG 147th Bde. R.F.A.

www.ingramcontent.com/pod-product-compliance
Lightning Source LLC
Chambersburg PA
CBHW081547160426
43191CB00011B/1860